LIVE THE BEST POSSIBLE LIFE BY SURVIVING MARRIAGE

LIVE THE BEST POSSIBLE LIFE BY SURVIVING MARRIAGE

A LIFE INSTRUCTION MANUAL

RICHARD MASON

BWM Books Pty Ltd
Canberra

Contents

Introduction vii
A shaky start on the way a top-quality marriage

Premise # 1 1
Yes, being married is required, if you are going to live the best life possible

Premise # 2 9
You can't tell someone how to have a great marriage unless you have one

Premise # 3 17
Marriage is a full partnership with no limited partners.

Premise #4 29
Sex is very important!!

Premise # 5 57
You must be fit to have a top-quality marriage, and live the best life possible

Premise # 6 75
You must be healthy

Premise # 7 93
You must have a healthy lifestyle

Premise # 8 97
Your appearance is a building block for a high-quality marriage

Premise # 9 115
Giving—as in gifts—will strengthen your marriage

Premise # 10 129
Kids are one of the building blocks of a high-quality marriage

Premise # 11 139
A marriage lived together is a prerequisite to a top-quality marriage

Premise # 12 151
Having a good-quality spiritual life is a building block to a great marriage

Premise # 13 161
To have a top-quality marriage you must compromise

Premise # 14 171
Talking is the thread that sews a marriage together

Premise # 15 187
Your marriage must have a foundation of honesty

Premise # 16 203
You can't have the best marriage and live the best life possible with a negative attitude

Premise # 17 209
In order to have a top-quality marriage, you must touch, hug, pat and embrace—you must be a serial toucher

Premise # 18 219
You must be your spouse's best friend

Premise # 19 227
You must pass this test with flying colors

Introduction

A shaky start on the way a top-quality marriage

I'm not shy. At least that's what most of my friends and enemies would say. In fact, when I stand to speak before a commission or the city council, I'm sure the chairman and council members hold their breath and expect to be raked over the coals. However, being an outspoken person and an extrovert is something I learned. It sure wasn't my nature when I was younger.

As a young boy, and later even as an adult, I was painfully shy. In high school, I never dated... not because I didn't want to, but because I was girl-shy. Even in college, I found it difficult to even stand before a class and give a report. I did finally start dating, but not very often. Just the idea of calling a girl on the phone, with the possibility that she would turn me down, kept me home most of the time.

When I met Vertis, I didn't call her for two weeks, and only by chance did I meet her at a local drive-in ice-cream place where many high school and college kids hung out. She drove up with several other girls, we started talking, and I asked her to go riding with a friend of mine and his girlfriend. We got in the back seat and talked for about 30 minutes. I wanted to ask her out on a real date, but I just couldn't get the words out of my mouth. Just before I got out of the car, though, I did ask her and held my breath until she said yes. As we began seeing each other, I would always ask for another date when I took her home.

We dated for a year, and then the following spring I graduated from the University of Arkansas with a B.S. degree in Geology. Because geology jobs were almost non-existent, I decided to return to college and get an advanced degree. That summer, I worked in a maintenance gang at a local refinery, and during that time, we decided to get married. We set the date for January 17, which was between semesters at the University of Arkansas. Our plan was for me to keep working through the fall to save up enough money for college, and at the end of the semester, we'd get married and both of us would go to college.

As our wedding day approached, I began to get nervous. Not because I didn't want to get married—it was my old shyness returning with a vengeance. Just the idea of standing in the front of a church full of people, with every eye on me, was enough to keep me from sleeping for almost a week before the ceremony.

The night before our wedding, Vertis and I sat in the balcony of the Rialto Theater in downtown El Dorado, Arkansas and watched Twenty Thousand Leagues Under The Sea. We cuddled and whispered to each other, sharing our plans for the life ahead of us. However, each time Vertis would say something like, "It's only sixteen hours until we'll be standing in the front of the church saying our wedding vows," my palms would begin to sweat, and I would become so nervous that it was hard for me to stay in my seat.

Our wedding day was a bright, cold January day. I had finally gotten over most of my nervousness about the wedding, but that would quickly change. I arrived at the church an hour before the wedding and waited around until my best man, my brother, and my five groomsmen arrived. I relaxed enough to kid around with Edward Lee McCall, one of the groomsmen.

"Hey, I wonder if anybody's gonna show up—Go take a look." Edward Lee slipped out the side door and peeked into the church auditorium. In a minute, he came back.

"It's packed! Even the balcony's full, and they're setting up extra seats down the aisle."

Some 500 relatives and friends had filled the church, and it was panic time again. By the time I walked out to stand in front of the congregation, my knees were shaking so much I could hardly walk. I just stood there, frozen in place. Edward Lee nudged me and said, "Smile—you look like you're at a funeral."

I did smile, but it was strained until Vertis started down the aisle. She looked so gorgeous that I relaxed—but only for a moment. I thought the wedding ceremony lasted for at least an hour and a half, but Vertis later told me it was only 20 minutes. I vividly remember walking out of the church, making our down the steps, and being hit by a hail of rice. Some of that rice—probably slung by my brother—was thrown so hard that it stung. However, we ducked our heads and plowed through the crowd to the car, we'd borrowed from Vertis's grandparents,—a car that was now slathered with shaving cream and decked out with tin cans tied on the back. We jumped in and roared off.

One block away, I stopped the car and removed the cans, and before we left town, we stopped at a 25-cent, do-it-yourself car wash to get the shaving cream off the car. Then it was off to a honeymoon in New Orleans by way of Ruston, Louisiana, where we were going to spend our first night together.

By the time we arrived at the Magnolia Motel in Ruston, we'd changed clothes, making an attempt to not to look like newlyweds. However, what happened next would prove to be one of the most embarrassing moments of my life.

I stopped well away from the check-in office at the motel, making sure the car— and Vertis—were far enough back to keep from being seen by the check-in clerk. I was wearing blue jeans and a pullover sweater, and in my mind, I'd planned to just casually stroll up like James Dean and check-in.

I walked into the office, dinged the little bell, and in a few minutes the clerk came out of the back room. It was a little, gray-haired, pleasant-looking lady who looked about 75. Everything was going fine. She smiled as she looked me over, and in my mind I could hear her thinking: Why is he here? Is he trying to hid something? Of course, she probably wasn't thinking anything, but I was beginning to get nervous again, and I was dreading any questions.

"Young man come over to the desk, and we'll get you checked in."

"Yes, mam." I tried to saunter over casually and even leaned one hand on the desk, as I waited for her to get the registration form.

"Do you have a reservation? Under what name?"

"Yes, mam. I'm Richard Mason. The reservation is just for tonight."

"Are you by yourself?"

"What?" I started to get a little panicky.

"Will you be the only person occupying the room?"

"Oh,—well, no mam—uh, well, my wife is with me."

"Your wife?"

"Yes, mam, she's in the car. It's parked in the lot over there. I'm a married man."

"It always nice to have a young married couple here. My husband and I have been married for over 50 years. How long have you been married?"

That question caught me so off-guard that I couldn't say anything for a few seconds. Finally, I managed to mumble something like, "Well, not that long." It must have sounded lame, because she looked at me, nodded her head, and began to grin.

"Well, let's see if I can find your reservation—Yes, here it is. Just sign on the bottom line, and I'll get your key."

Finally, I thought, and I began to relax again, thinking she would just hand me a key and that would be it. But it wasn't. I took the pen and leaned over to sign the check-in form. Then something happened that still makes me grin. (However, as a shy young man of 22, the little problem didn't seem funny right then.) The problem was caused by the most popular guy's hairstyle of the day— a flattop. That was my look of the moment, and, since I had fine black hair, I had to put a lot of flattop wax on to make it stand up.

When I leaned over to sign the check-in form, some wedding rice fell out of my hair and onto the desk. I jerked back as soon as I saw the first grains hit the table, but that was exactly the wrong thing to do. It caused a torrent—at least to me—of rice to pelt the table. I tried to sweep away the grains and sign my name at the same time, but as you might know, I signed the wrong line. I jerked around trying to get it right and more rice peppered down. Of course, with every grain, I kept trying to sign my name. I finally managed to scribble g a signature.

Well, the nice lady held back a laugh when the first grains of rice hit. I guess she couldn't figure it out, but as the rice kept raining down, she realized what was happening, and she let out a giggle, which quickly turned in to a real hee-haw. My face must have been beet-red as I tried to explain about just getting married. She laughed until tears ran down her cheeks, then she finally produced a key, and Vertis and I began our marriage.

The next day, we drove to New Orleans for our honeymoon, and 50-years later, we returned to where it all started. However, this time we didn't stay at a Quality Inn for $8 a night and eat 15-cent Krystal hamburgers.

On the way back home, after reminiscing about our life together, I began to think about the remarkable quality of our marriage. It was those thoughts that brought me to a decision to share some of what I think are universal qualities that make a great marriage. I believe that, without a doubt, my wife and I have a marriage and a life that if measured against the norm would put us in the 95th percentile of happy couples.

This life manual is my attempt to explain why and how to have a top marriage, and in doing so live the best life available to you.

Premise # 1

Yes, being married is required, if you are going to live the best life possible

I'm sure many single individuals, and quite a few married ones, will immediately object when they glance at the title of this chapter.

"What? You've got to be married to live the best life possible? You're kidding!"

Well, I guess, if this book is going to have any validity, I must answer this two-part question: "Why would a person even want to be married, much less actually survive marriage—you know—"till death do you part?" And if two people do have a top- quality marriage, are they really living the best life possible?"

I'll try to answer at least the first question in this chapter, but the second question is the whole premise of the book, and I hope by the time you finish reading, you'll have the answers.

To answer the first question, we must understand that almost everything we do in this old world has a risk-rewards relationship. It's a basic trait ingrained in human nature to pursue things in life that offer more "pros" than "cons" or to put it another way, things that give us more pleasure or satisfaction. We essentially live life guided by that inclination.

Now, let's apply the pursuit of pleasure to marriage. When we weigh out the pros and cons, the bad and the good, is it worth it to be married? Is a married life better than being single? Will a quality marriage really enable you to live the best life possible? Yes, of course, I believe so, or I wouldn't have spent time writing this book. Now, let's examine why, but let's make the premise more straightforward: If you do survive marriage and live together unto "death do you part," have you lived the best life possible? Would you have been better off just to have remained single and lived your life without a companion?

To answer that question, I've examined not only my own life and marriage, but numerous others, all the way to the end of their lives. And this is my conclusion: I believe being married is the only way to obtain the highest level of satisfaction in life. If you're not married, you can't possibly have the infinite number of positive emotional responses available to a married couple. That premise has been proven to be true by not only my observations, but by hundreds of marriage studies.

Yes, I'm sure many people live pleasant, enjoyable lives, and they aren't married. However, they're going to be shortchanged in life because they can never experience the pleasures and emotional satisfaction available in a good marriage. Each one may live a good life, but not the best life possible.

In order to understand the value of a good marriage, we must look around and examine marriage, and not just my marriage (which we'll look into in detail) but also the marriages of other couples who are still hanging on and happily surviving.

Well, there's no doubt a lot of couples who take seriously the promise of "till death do us part" in the marriage vows. But judging by some awfully sad faces, and just what you hear at the grocery store about old so-in-so's marriage, things aren't that rosy in a lot of marriages. It's pretty obvious that many couples aren't living the best life possible.

Yes, I believe millions of couples are surviving marriage, but are actually in failed relationships. They're together, but at what cost? Clearly, in my opinion, the cons in these marriages far outweigh the pros, and, without a doubt, many of these couples are staying together for reasons other than the joy and contentment of a successful marriage. They are not, by any stretch of the imagination, living the best life available to them! Their marriage has failed, and they just haven't pulled the plug. (I, personally, believe that divorce is a better option for the people in those marriages, Living a single life or remarrying is preferable to living in a failed relationship.)

So let me make one thing very clear: Surviving marriage successfully is more than just staying together. My definition, the one I will refer to in this book, is not only just staying married, but having a quality, long-term relationship that puts a couple in the 95th percentile of all marriages. In other words, my premise is that these couples are not only surviving marriage; they are living the best life available to them.

Naturally, all of us would like to be in that select group of married couples, but it's a sad fact that most marriages are less than they could be. All couples want a top-quality marriage, but it seems most won't put in the effort to reach that goal And why don't they? It might help us understand why, and how to reach the ultimate marriage and live the best life possible, by revisiting the single vs. married proposition.

First, let's consider living your life without a live-in companion. You're single. I'm sure all of us can point out single individuals who seem to be living a great life,; it's not all doom and gloom if you're not married. But let's face it: Singleness is not the natural order of things. That's right—hear me out. It's not the natural order of things.

The deeper we look into human behavior, the more we see marriage as a natural order that has been proven over time to be the best way to live the fullest and most pleasurable life. And you don't have to dig very deep to hit the facts. To start with: Married couples live longer. Many studies indicate that there is something about marriage that extends life. Not only does marriage apparently extend life, but according to a new study, married couples have a much lower incidence of dementia and Alzheimer's than do singles. Put those two together, and you get not only a longer life, but a longer, higher-quality life.

I don't think any of us ever would want to get married, though, in order to just live longer. To be honest, you can't put your finger on any one thing that makes marriage a positive way to live. If we knew all the details of our physical and mental framework, I'm sure we'd be shocked to find out that there are hundreds of reasons why marriage works. And to further complicate things, every marriage is different, and the emotional framework of each marriage is unlike any other.

But all successful marriages have one simple thing in common: The top- quality relationships are the ones where the marriage partners work together to make the union work. That's the key word—work. If you're not ready to invest time, energy, and yes, even some extra money in a marriage, then this book is not for you. Very few marriages just click, and if you're newly married and expect to drive off into the sunset and live happily ever after—without any effort—then you'll probably be disappointed.

This book is written on the premise that most marriage partners go through a lot tears, anguish, and stress before they reach a quality plateau. The ones who work together to survive marriage, and learn from those experiences, are the ones who will benefit from this book. Tucked away in these 200 or so pages are little gems of wisdom that will improve your marriage and your life, but they'll only work if both parties in the marriage are committed. The idea is not to just hang in there and hope for the best, but to work collectively and move up to a plateau which probably less than 5% of all couples ever reach.

So my goal is to help your marriage to not only work, but to improve until you are living the most satisfying and pleasurable life you can have. In this country over 40% of all marriages end in divorce. That number is shamefully high, and it's high, for one reason, because so many couples are not willing to work together to make a successful marriage. These couples take marriage so lightly that the smallest problems can cause a trip to the divorce court.

Not only do we have a high percentage of all marriages ending up in divorce, but countless others never reach their potential. They're like the movie that begins wonderfully, but instead of soaring, flops or struggles along and finally ends with a whimper.

This book wasn't written to keep every marriage together, because some marriages aren't worth saving—they're mistakes, and if you're in a hopeless marriage, my best advice is to get out. The goal of this book is to help marriages that have potential to reach an extraordinary marriage plateau that will enable the couples to live the best life available to them. I believe the guidelines in this book, if incorporated into your marriage, will move you up into the elite 95th percentile of all marriages in the country.

It's not easy, but if you could —have the best life possible, wouldn't it be worth any effort you could make to get there? Of course, it would, and you would expend whatever energy, money, or time it took to reach that marriage plateau. So roll up your sleeves, and get ready to put some effort into something that will greatly improve your life.

I believe, for a marriage to be successful and thrive, it takes a great deal of love, commitment, and plain old hard work. And because of the complex relationships that evolve in a marriage, it is impossible to focus on just one aspect of the marriage. Anyone who tells you to just get -________ right, (fill in the blank,) and you'll have a successful marriage is unbelievably naive.

A marriage is made up of two complex organisms who are ever-changing and are always surprising each other in their emotional relationship. That's why understanding and flexibility must be the key you work on marriage problems. The two words "understanding and flexibility" will be repeated over and over again, because these actions are critical when you deal with the intricate nature of marriage.

Yes, marriage is complex, and emotions within marriage are particularly complicated. That's why I'll cover many points that work together to produce a quality marriage. To have the kind of high-quality marriage and life I'm writing about requires a dedication and commitment from both parties, and, for your marriage to succeed, it requires a focus on every relationship item outlined in this book—not just one or two key points.

I believe there's a level of marriage that exists which most couples never attain. It's available to all, but it's the rare couple who will commit enough mental and sometimes physical energy to reach that level. That superior level is what this book is all about, and the premise is not that you will have a perfect marriage, because that's impossible, but that you will reach a level of contentment and pleasure that allows you to live life to the fullest.

But for a moment let's go back to why you would want to even be married. Marriages can be complex and bewildering. So why would a person willingly become involved in such a relationship? The answer is simple: A knock-'em-dead marriage is the most satisfying relationship imaginable. When it's right it's unbelievably good, but when it's bad it's hell. If you're reading this book, your marriage is probably somewhere between "hell and passable." You're the reader who should devour this book, because you are missing living the best life possible.

I'm writing this book while enjoying the best possible marriage relationship, myself. It's not only good, it astonishes me every day. However, it didn't happen overnight, and I'd be lying if I told you our marriage has been a bed of roses. We've had our up and downs, but over the years Vertis and I have figured out a few things that make a marriage work, and if I can pass these common-sense secrets on to you, then it will have been worth my effort to write this book.

So, before you jump into the next chapter, make up your mind that a good marriage is worth saving and enjoying. And if something has worth, then it is rarely easy to achieve. Having an out-of-this-world marriage—in which you can live the best live available to you—won't be the easiest thing you've ever done, but if you succeed it will be well worth the effort.

Before I close this chapter, let me give you a little scientific evidence that may encourage you to work on your marriage.

A recent CNN online article stated it this way: "A recent study by Linda Waite, a sociologist at the University of Chicago, and co-author Mary Elizabeth Hughes of Johns Hopkins Bloomberg School of Public Health, found divorced or widowed people have 20 percent more chronic health conditions such as heart disease, diabetes, or cancer than married people. They also have 23 percent more mobility limitations, such as trouble climbing stairs or walking a block."

CNN also quotes one of the authors, Linda Waite: "Divorced people have more chronic conditions, more mobility limitations, and rate their health as poorer than people like them in age, race, gender, education, who've been married once and are still married."

Another study by Mark Hayward, director of the Population Research Center and a Professor of Sociology Fellow at the University of Texas, confirms these conclusions. His 2006 study, funded by the National Institute on Aging, found that divorced, middle-aged women were 60% more likely to have cardiovascular disease than middle-aged women who remain married.

Mark Hayward put it this way: "There's no erasure of the effects of divorce. There is intense stress leading up to divorce and stresses during divorce proceedings. Think of divorce as one of the most intense stressors. It leads to what we call dysregulation, [impairment] in key cardiovascular process that may be permanently altered. You're not going back to your original set point."

But there's another reason to be married, and this one is financial. In a Associated Press article, David Crary cites a recent study by the Pew Research Center that points out, among other things, that married men are much more financially secure, primarily because of having more working wives. To quote the article, "One barometer is median household income—which rose 60 percent between 1970 and 2007 for married men and married women, but only 16 percent for unmarried men, according to the Pew data."

The reason is that in 1970 only 4 percent of working wives made more than their husbands, while in 2007, 22 percent made more than their working husbands. The obvious conclusion is that being married usually makes an individual more financially secure.

Enough said?

Well, maybe saving that wounded marriage is worthwhile after all. I hope you'll agree, and, as you read this book, resolve to work with your marriage partner to try these keys to improving your relationship. If you do, you can reach that magical 95th percentile and live the most enjoyable life available to you.

Premise # 2

You can't tell someone how to have a great marriage unless you have one

My Marriage

Well, I guess you would expect the author of this book to be a Ph.D. with a string of degrees, but this one isn't. Oh, I have a few degrees, but I don't think Bachelor's and Master's degrees in Geology give me much of a professional background as a counselor. And my profession sure doesn't have anything to do with how to survive and prosper in a marriage relationship. However, you could say I'm well "Home-Schooled" in marriage counseling.

My ideas about how to have a quality marriage are very simple, and this illustration might help to explain it. Several years ago we built our dream house: a big redwood-and-glass house on a densely, wooded lot sitting on the edge of a small lake. We worked with our architect to have everything we could imagine built-in. It took more than a year to build.

Our job foreman, Jack Hampton, didn't have a degree in anything that would relate to homebuilding. In fact, Jack had only graduated from high school, but he was not only a master carpenter, he was a whiz at function, structure, and design. All of which had come from his 30 years of experience in building homes. He'd become a building professional—from experience.

During the building of our house, Jack would frequently call me over to point out problems. Sometimes they were real mistakes; others times they were minor glitches, things that our architect had overlooked. It wasn't because our architect didn't do a good job, it's just the way things are when you build a house. Little things pop up that no one expects.

Jack, however, would always have a solution. He would point out the problem, and then say in his deep, south Arkansas drawl, "Well, Mr. Mason, if it was my house I would do…" It didn't take long for me to realize that Jack knew from experience how to solve house-building problems. He was never wrong, and I usually nodded my head "yes" before he even finished the sentence.

Jack's on-the-job experience is like this manual on marriage. I believe I have some insight into solving many of the common problems that plague the average married couple. Just like Jack knew how to build houses, I believe I know how to build a great marriage—from experience.

If you think our 50-year marriage has been a bed of roses, think again. We're highly emotional individuals who hit the speed bumps of life at full throttle. Of course, that sometimes made our life more exciting and fulfilling, but not all the time. In the past we've collided countless times and we've come out of those collisions with some bruised egos and a plenty of regrets. (Yes, we certainly regret some of those yelling, screaming, and pouting fusses.)

I know you may be scratching your head as you read about our marriage being anything but perfect. No, we do not have a perfect marriage—no one does. As you read this book, I want you to understand that surviving marriage and living the best life possible isn't being lovey-dovey 24 hours a day or living in uninterrupted bliss. No! That would be so boring no one would want to survive marriage. The marriage I believe is worth striving for will still have its bumps and emotional swings, but overall, it will be a deeply fulfilling relationship that will sustain and enrich your life—and enable you to live the best life possible.

The relationship ride that begins with saying "I do" will take you through emotional valleys and to mountaintops, but remember that you can never have the mountaintop experiences without the valleys. Another example: This time in Switzerland. We lived overseas for several years and had the opportunity to visit that scenic county numerous times. Of course, everyone who's ever traveled to Switzerland remembers the majestic snow-covered peaks, and, as most people view these peaks, they suppose they're some of the tallest mountains in the world. But there're not. What makes those mountains look so high are the deep valleys. And it's the same way with a marriage. Difficult marriage valleys, which are followed by marriage peaks, make a marriage surge with emotion—You can't have the high marriage mountains without the valleys of despair. So remember that if you're going through a marriage valley; the emotional mountain is ahead of you, if you persevere.

My purpose is to tell you how to survive the roller-coaster ride we call marriage, and in surviving reach a level where not only are you surviving, but you're living the best life possible with someone who's your best friend. And if making your spouse your best friend isn't something you really want to do right now, stick with this book, and maybe you'll see why it will be the best thing you've ever done!

But, before we go any further, let's get one thing straight: Not everyone is going to follow my so-called marriage guidelines, and no matter how hard you try some partners will be a real pain when it comes to certain items within a marriage. When that happens—after you have given it your best shot—weigh the pluses and minuses, and if he or she comes up short time after time, consider divorcing him or her. Don't live a miserable life with someone just because you don't want to get a divorce, or for the kids, or your parents, or whatever the reason. Life is too short to live with someone who makes your life miserable. This book is not meant to be a "Hold it together at all costs manual." This book is to make two lovers as happy as they can be while living together in an imperfect world, and in doing so live the best life possible.

Vertis and I have built a 50-year relationship, which I think is remarkable. We started our marriage when we were young, 17 and 22, headstrong and emotional. We never went to a marriage counselor because we never considered our marriage in trouble. Of course, our marriage went through some rocky times, as almost everyone's does, but for some reason, we stayed together and muddled through our problems, learning not to make the same mistake twice.

One of our biggest problems turned out to be our similar emotional backgrounds, and our desire to be independent people. Boy, early on, we really did butt heads as we tried to "do our own thing"—many times at the expense of our partner. And sometimes we reached the point where doing our own thing was becoming so destructive to our marriage, and making our lives so miserable, that we realized it, and one or the other quit.

What we did find, as our marriage matured, was that the closeness and intimacy we were building strengthened our relationship; and, as that happened, our marriage and life together became more enjoyable. Over the years we've continued to build on the foundation of intimacy we initiated when we were in our 20s, and today actually, it's not just today, but for at least the last 25 years—we've become so close and connected that we react as one. We think alike, love the same things, and are excited when one or the other excels in whatever they're doing.

Finally, the crux of the matter: We are extremely content in our relationship, and we believe we're living the best life we could possible live. It's hard to write about how our relationship weathered the frequent storms of marriage and turned out so positive because some of those times were painful and strained our relationship. Occasionally, in the past, we've struggled just to stay together, but today we are still married because we're having the time of our lives, and we believe that the on-the-job training we've gone through for the past 50 years is something that should be shared with other struggling couples. In a nutshell, we want to share the secrets of a quality marriage, and how to achieve the best life available.

However, this book is less of a book about deep marriage secrets than it is a practical guide to building a relationship that will not only hold a marriage together, but help it continually improve as it ages, resulting in the most satisfying life possible. As I mentioned earlier, a marriage relationship is so complicated that it's impossible to focus on only one part of that relationship. And as I prepared to write this book, I spent quite a while forging some of the keys to a successful marriage. The chapters in this book focus on some of the more important individual aspects of marriage, but because there are so many variations in the emotional bonds that exist between couples, there could have easily been twice as many chapters.

Each of these chapters outlines one important aspect of the marriage. These are the building blocks of a quality marriage, and they have not only stood the test of time, but they have been proven to be fulfilling and immeasurably helpful in nurturing a marriage.

To me, marriage is such an important and integral part of life that living in a marriage that is not fulfilling has got to be one of the saddest, most miserable experiences in life. Most events have a start and ending, but with a marriage it's never-ending. If the misery is there, it will most likely be there tomorrow and for as long as you stay with your spouse. That's the primary reason for spending time and energy to a pleasurable and satisfying relationship. Why live a miserable life when, with a little work, an infinitely better relationship is available?

In this book I'll take you through our relationship, and I won't cover up or skim over the problems we've encountered during our marriage. But I will show you how we overcame them, and how we emerged from those problem times more committed and happier than ever.

It's a sad fact that many couples today aren't willing to expend the energy to survive marriage. They take the easy way out—divorce—which has pervaded our society until we're faced with the fact that so many marriages end in divorce. These couples chose going back to an inferior life as a single person instead of working to raise the relationship to a better level. They're making a terrible choice when they choose divorce rather than working to achieve a good-quality marriage.

Yes, Vertis and I had to work to bring our marriage up to the level it is today, and over the years we had problem after problem that we solved together. Of course solving those problems was a lot harder to do than to talk or write about them. We all know a few words that will send our spouse into a fit of anger—and, boy, do we ever have to watch it when tempers began to rise, and we're tempted to throw out an old girlfriend or boyfriend' name, or mention that little muffin top someone has picked up over the past few years. To relish those hateful, destructive, "cuss-fights," can turn a marriage into a continuous battleground and ultimately lead to divorce—or worse—living in a failed marriage.

Yes, those bad, unforgiving marriages can be a rough road, where bumps are constant, but they don't have to be. Make a commitment to build quality, and you can have the marriage, and life, we all strive for.

If you think you're going to read a book here about a couple who solved all their marriage problems and are now living a perfect marriage, you're going to be disappointed. On the other hand, if you're looking for ways to improve your lives together, and are willing to apply some of the principals that have made my own marriage what it is today, then you acquire the keys to a contented and happy life.

Vertis is, quite frankly, my lover, my best friend, my counselor, my dietitian, my physical trainer, and almost anything else you can think of. Of course, the same applies to my relationship with her, and that's what this book is all about. Every marriage is a struggle to reach the ultimate level of contentment available to a couple, and it can only be done by becoming your spouse's best friend.

How do you get to that level—and more important, is it worth it when you get there? Of course! In my opinion, it's worth all the stress, work, and money, because it's the most joyous and pleasurable life possible. As far as I'm concerned, it's the best life Vertis and Richard could possibly live.

Premise # 3

Marriage is a full partnership with no limited partners.

A Partnership

A high-quality marriage is a partnership and that partnership is not a master-servant relationship. Yes, I know what Paul said in his letter to the church at Corinth, but Paul was talking about social conditions in the first century. He also wrote about a slave-master relationship that has disappeared with time. Today, things have changed, and if you're going to have a top-quality, compatible relationship in today's stress-filled, complicated world, it had better be one where the spouses are equal partners, with no managing partner. Believe me, if that's not the case, your marriage will never reach its full potential.

Of course, that seems to fly in the face of tradition and common sense—like a ship with no captain—but not really. Carefully analyze any successful marriage and I think you'll find, that whether the partners realize it or not, most of the time they act in a partnership fashion, because each spouse brings to the table certain strengths. It may be that the wife, in some cases, is the primary breadwinner and the husband is in charge of the kitchen. It can work both ways, and there is no right way; both are right.

But let's go back to this so-called partnership. Can a marriage work when no one is in charge? Yes, but first we need to get rid of the phrase "In Charge." That gives the wrong connotation. What I believe makes a marriage partnership function well is when the strengths of each partner are used to their fullest. Of course, we all agree with that statement, but how do we use each partner's strengths to enhance a marriage?

Actually it's simple. When questions come up that relate to the strength of one partner's expertise, the other partner acquiesces. It's not a "roll-over-and-play dead" move while the other partner takes charge of whatever the situation is; it's letting the best and most competent marriage partner solve that particular problem. The logic is overwhelming. Shouldn't the partner who is the most competent in that subject be the one the marriage partners rely on? Yes, of course—that is, if you want the best outcome. Anytime a marriage partner, tries to solve a problem, and that partner has the lesser capabilities, then the marriage will suffer.

Can you imagine a business that didn't use the capabilities of its employees to the company's best advantage? It doesn't make sense in the business world, and it doesn't make any sense in a marriage.

However, as in any situation, certain things come up which are in gray areas. Sometimes, for example, both partners are close to being equal in ability. It's these areas where the marriage partnership comes under stress, especially if one partner has a strong objection to what the other partner is recommending. Naturally, comprise is the solution, and that must be sought after diligently. But sometimes a comprise is not possible, and when there is a firm "No" on one side of the decision and a equally firm "Yes" on the other, the situation must be considered a stalemate, and left unresolved until there is a change of heart by someone. A headstrong "I know best" attitude, where one partner bulls his or her way ahead, is a sure recipe for future marriage problems.

I know that setting up a household, handling finances and kids, and managing all that goes with marriage seems like an impossible job, especially when the marriage is operating under a partnership arrangement. So just how do you set up a household where it takes a unanimous vote to do anything? Well, the first thing you do is to set some rules; and the first rule you set is—"rules are made to be broken." That's right; break a few rules along the way, because one of the things that creates more marriages problems than anything else, is rigidity. Don't be stubborn over the little stuff but realize this: Most couples cope with the few massive upheavals that hit a marriage, only to break down when the little daily, nit-picking destroys the very emotional fabric which holds a marriage together. Little insignificant compromises along the way grease the wheels of a successful marriage.

Take some time to listen to others talk about their marriage problems. You'll immediately realize, that most of their problems seem insignificant. They're little things that one marriage partner can't let go of. If you go through many years of marriage, you'll find out that almost everything is little stuff, and the folks who get upset—and stay upset—because of minor irritations are the folks who get divorces.

I firmly believe that most divorces, when analyzed in detail, aren't caused by big events that devastated the marriage. No, most divorces are caused by dozens of small, insignificant problems that build until one of the partners calls it quits.

But let's be practical and not just talk in theory. After all, we're imperfect humans, and in a marriage relationship little imperfections are impossible to hide. But when two people love each other and want to accommodate the other's desires, then they have a working platform to build on. That's the cardinal rule. Love has got to be there or forget marriage.

Below I have listed some rules that apply to a successful marriage partnership.

Rule (1): Marriage is for lovers, so if you can barely abide your spouse, don't plan to stay together. However, if once upon a time, you did love your spouse, then there's hope. After all, sometimes love in marriage is like a campfire that once was blazing and now is down to embers. If those embers are stoked and tended too, they will blaze again—and so will love in a marriage, if it is nurtured.

Now, let's assume you've passed the love test. How do you proceed?

First, you must be aware of each other's strengths and weakness. In every marriage, certain daily tasks and responsibilities naturally gravitate toward the spouse who is more capable of handling them—if you let them. However, if you're a control freak, and must be in charge of everything, then the tasks that should have gone to your spouse will be poorly done, causing stress in the marriage. Let's look at an example; if you're terrible with finances, then, unless your partner is worse than you, he or she should be the one who handles the money. Okay, you see conflict coming when Mr. So-in-So, doles out your allowance and it doesn't include enough for your shoe habit. Problem? You bet it is, if Mr. So-in-So acts as Father Superior and doesn't allow input about how the partnership money is to be spent. Is there enough money for shoes? Is my shoe habit unreasonable?

Unless there's openness and a transparency in the financial part of the marriage, there'll inevitably be stress and conflict. However, apply the partnership rule in this case: When the managing financial partner can, in good conscious, produce an unbiased budget, and the shoe expenses are clearly out of line, then that partner is justified in complaining about the shoe expenditure, and the other individual should be satisfied.

Rule 2: It's everyone's money, not just the one who brings home the bigger paycheck. The marriage partner who stays home and takes care of hundreds of little or big items actually earns an equal share of the entire partnership money, and is entitled to respect. If the partner who understands finances and brings home the paycheck, tries to make all the decisions about how the joint money will be spent, then trouble is brewing. Our country has passed the time when the male was always the breadwinner, and we lived in a patriarchal society. Today, for the male in the partnership to assert he has the right to direct every activity in the marriage is just as wrong as saying women shouldn't have the right to vote.

I think we all agree with the above statement, but how do you keep male dominance from happening, and why is that such a bad thing? Look at it this way: The very last thing you want in a marriage is for only one partner to have an understanding of the financial assets and liabilities. Maybe you hate dealing with money, and you had rather he or she would just tell you how much you can spend this month, or how much should be save, or which stocks to invest in. That's a horrible plan, and, if you handle your finances in that manner, one day you'll regret it.

What if your husband or wife of 25 years runs off with his or her administrative assistant and cleans out every bit of cash the family has saved? Or a more likely scenario is that when he or she dies someday, you'll be faced with trying to manage a financial portfolio without any experience. Either way, you're in a mess, a mess that you could have prevented if you'd only learned a little more about the family finances.

This is how an ideal marriage partnership should run on a financial level. First, as we mentioned before, it's everyone's money. Let's just say for the sake of argument, though, that the wife has a better head for finances than the husband. If this couple is smart, she'll be given the primary responsibility for balancing the checkbook, taking care of tax returns, and other handling other strictly financial matters. However, when it comes to household items and personal expenditures, then those decisions become strictly joint decisions, and if Joe Blow goes out and buys a bass boat for $15,000, without even mentioning it to his wife and blowing the budget, then he violated one of the key precepts of the marriage.

If Joe does something that stupid, then obviously he doesn't have a clue whether or not the marriage partnership can afford a boat. He just wants one, and he rationalizes they can afford it. What should have happened was for Joe to have been brought along by his wife until he understood the limits of what they could or could not do. Secondly, he violated the trust of the partnership, by unilaterally doing something that dramatically disrupted the trust created within a marriage, and doing so put the marriage under stress and maybe in financial danger.

You don't do things like that to your best friend.

Maybe this sounds simple, but the only way to make a joint financial commitment in a marriage is to lay everything out on the table—and not after the fact. If old Joe was planning to buy the bass boat, but didn't even mention it to his wife, he violated this basic premise of a marriage partnership.

In an ideal best case, financial matters should be a part of your everyday conversation. The grocery bill, car payments, stock purchases, and dozens of other financial matters should be routinely discussed, and, yes, debated. If the subject of a bass boat had been put on the table and discussed, Joe would have probably understood that buying it would be disastrous for the family budget, and he wouldn't have proceeded—unless he was a real jerk.

In an ideal marriage you should seek a consensuses in everything. Most of the time, after a few years of togetherness, couples reach compatibility. Let me make myself clear: I'm talking about being totally attuned to your spouse in every aspect of your marriage. In Chapter Four, I'll discuss sexual compatibility, but at this juncture I want to mention the second biggest problem that most couples face—being financially compatible. A recent article in The New York Times covered the problem quite well.

"It seems research has shown most individuals prefer to marry someone with similar spending attitudes. However, when it comes to marriage, many times spendthrifts marry tightwads. It doesn't make any sense, but for some reason these financial opposites seem to attract. If we look at the basic traits of a spendthrift and a tightwad, I think we can see why these marriages have many more problems than other marriages where the couples are closer to being the same in their financial outlook. A spendthrift experiences too little pain when spending, leading them to spend more than they should. Tightwads, by contrast, report feeling too much pain when spending. They have trouble parting with their pennies." (The New York Times, Aug. 15, 2009)

Of course, it doesn't take a genius to see how this incompatibility, when it comes to marriage, would lead to constant bickering. And it certainly shouldn't surprise you that financially mismatched couples have a much higher divorce rate than ones who are more compatible.

Researchers have found that couples tend to avoid discussing sex and financial matters the most. They say, "We're in love!" and expect everything to go smoothly. However, since sex and finances are major factors in any marriage, discussing them should be a high priority.

Let me be clear: If marriage is to work, financial compatibility is extremely helpful, but not absolutely necessary. However, for the partnership to work under less than ideal conditions, then the couple must be a willing to compromise and to recognize the inherent problems that confront them. If they have an open relationship about financial matters, and are willing to work diligently to be responsive to income and expenses, then I believe such a partnership could work. (Setting up rules that both agree to abide by, however, and write them down. That is a good start.)

Even for couples who are financially compatible, however, money is still one of the primary causes of martial rifts. All of us have experienced headaches associated with money and marriage. So how do we minimize the stress involved by trying to budget limited funds when confronted with almost unlimited desires? Of course, if those desires were the same for both parties, then our problem would be a whole lot simpler, but many times our wants are far apart. In fact, there are times when one spouse will be passionate about purchasing something the other absolutely detests. How in the world can a marriage that requires unanimous decision-making handle that?

The first thing to remember is that if this equal partnership is to work, then you must keep the unanimous decision part. Of course, Betty Sue is adamantly against Joe purchasing the boat, and after she shows Joe what the purchase would do to their finances, we would hope Joe would see the light—and maybe he would. However, most purchases aren't whoppers like a bass boat, so it's the little things, again, that bedevil a marriage. For example, how about Betty Sue's new shoes?

"What? Three-hundred and fifty-dollars for a pair of high heels?" You can just hear him now, can't you? Well, you say, so much for a unanimous decision. Maybe not, because old Joe knows, if he turns down the shoes, he'd better be ready when Betty Sue vetoes the new $350-dollar fishing rod. So it's a trade-off isn't it? Yes, that's what marriage is all about; it's a trade-off for the benefit of both. If old Joe smiles, nods, and blesses the shoes, then Betty Sue is going to be thrilled, and I'll guarantee you she'll be a lot easier to live with—and Joe will get his new fishing rod.

Before we go to the next chapter, let's discuss trading off in a little more detail. Sometimes a marriage partner has to give up something that to him or her is not threatening to the marriage, but which the other thinks is very destructive. With an issue like that, the first partner must make the decision to give up whatever is causing the problem within the marriage, even if it is something he or she wants very much. For that partner not to be responsive would weaken the marriage substantially, and create a festering emotional boil which will someday explode into a marriage threatening crisis. Defuse such problems or else no marriage "how to" book is going to help.

Let me give you an example of a problem that occurred in my marriage.

Back when I was in college, I began playing poker, first with a summer hay-bailing crew, then in a college dorm, and later in several fraternity houses. By the time I was a junior, I'd developed into a better-than-average, college-level poker player. Then, the summer after my junior year, I worked on an offshore drilling rig in the Gulf of Mexico, playing poker almost every day with some Cajun whizzes, and by the time I started my senior year of college I could really clean up on the fraternity house circuit. I bought my first car that year, an old 1950 Ford, with poker winnings.

After Vertis and I married, graduated, and moved to Kingsville, Texas, to work, I continued to play an occasional poker game with some of the other geologists and engineers in the office. I won almost every time. After two years of working in Kingsville, I took a transfer to Benghazi, Libya, to do well-site work for Exxon in the Libyan Desert. Well, being out for 14 days at a time, with very little to do, put me in a non-stop poker game with some of the best poker players I'd ever played with. For a while I was getting nicked pretty hard, but after a few months of almost continual playing, I was holding my own, and when I transferred back to the states two years later, I was almost unbeatable. I'd become a stellar poker player.

The poker playing that caused our marriage problems occurred when we'd been back in the states for a few months. I'd joined a weekly poker game with geologists and engineers I worked with. My poker playing experience put me head and shoulders above anyone in the game, and, unless I had a unusual streak of bad luck, I routinely walked away with several hundred dollars in winnings every time I played. After a few months of playing every Friday night, I began to get a hint that something was wrong.

Every time I returned home and pulled out a wad of bills that I'd won, I detected an attitude from Vertis that all was not well. Of course, I was only thinking about adding to my meager salary and maybe buying a new car with my winnings. However, Vertis looked at it differently. We were close friends with almost the entire poker-playing bunch, and they were in about the same financial shape we were: newly married, just out of college, and trying to get by on an entry-level salary.

Vertis did not object to my playing on moral grounds or because I was away from her one night a week. Instead, she could see that my winnings were cutting into the take-home-pay of many of our friends. If I was out of the game, then the winners were spread around the table and no one was hurt.

As the weeks passed, Vertis became really upset every time I left to play poker, and when I came home I tried to hide my winnings. (Trying to hide several hundred dollars in quarters and small bills in a small house where your wife is by your side every minute, won't work. I can speak from experience.)

After a few more weeks, I knew I had a decision to make. I'd either quit the game forever, or have an extremely disruptive problem in our marriage. It was a tough decision for me, because not only was I winning but I also dearly loved to play poker; and not only that, but I really enjoyed the banter with my fellow workers. I thought about it for about a week, and then, the next Friday night—our regular poker playing night—I asked Vertis out to dinner to a great seafood restaurant. Of course, she knew I always played poker on Friday nights, so she immediately asked me what was going on.

"I'm not playing poker anymore," I said. "I've quit."

I know Vertis felt guilty about wanting me to quit, but, after a mild protest, she smiled, hugged me, and almost broke into tears. Until that moment I hadn't realized how important my acquiescence was to her. That gesture did a lot to strengthen our marriage ties.

I learned an important marriage principal that day. If you want to build up the emotional marriage bond between you and your spouse, give up something for the other. It can be a bad habit, one you know your spouse just tolerates, or it can be an action where un-thoughtfulness is replaced by thoughtfulness.

Maybe you need to return to a "dating" mood where you were solicitous to his or her every need. You opened the car door for her, or touched and hugged him, for one reason, you were wooing. The wooing is over, but the emotional surge that these actions created is still available to couples who want to strengthen their marriage. If you will consciously work to change the things your spouse dislikes in your lifestyle, it will bring about a positive change in the emotional attitude of your spouse. Every time you give up something for your spouse, you move closer to having a quality marriage.

Creating a true marriage partnership a big step toward making it to that 95th percentile, but unless you achieve this kind of partnership in your marriage, you can never live the best life possible.

Premise #4
Sex is very important!!

Is Sex The Marriage Super Glue?

Yes, in some cases it is, but, in spite of everything you read or see on TV, sex can only do so much for a marriage. Sex isn't everything.

However, don't minimize it, either. It's damn important. Let's face it, sex is the basic reason for a marriage. Without sex, you don't have a full marriage relationship, and to reach the quality marriage plateau we're striving for, a top-notch sex life is an absolute must.

As you get into this chapter, you'll realize it's much longer than any of the other chapters. Well, I didn't intend it to be, but as I wrote it, there seemed to be a lot to say about sex. In fact, as I went over all the other items that go into a quality marriage, I realized sex is the linchpin. Without a superior sexual experience in a relationship, you can't possibly have an off-the-charts marriage. And there are so many sexual curves in the road, so to speak, that addressing all of them takes a lot more paper than the other chapters.

But let's get back to sex as the glue. Is that valid? Let me be completely honest with you. Over the years, especially when Vertis and I were going through some rocky times, I think sex kept our marriage together. There were occasions when one of us was ready to give up and walk out, and on some of those times, our sex life literally saved a struggling marriage. Sex can't always save a floundering marriage, but it can push the reset button, especially if you're very sexually compatible.

Of course, the place for in a marriage varies with each couple, and as we'll see later in this chapter, the frequency of sexual relations depends upon the couple. However, if sex is strained, forced, or too infrequent for one of the parties, that couple will surely have problems; they're almost certainly faced with a sub-par relationship.

Yes, sex is a glue, but it is not always a super glue, and just a good sex life won't assure you a good marriage. Sometimes other marriage problems are so overwhelming that a good sex life is pushed into the background. I've known couples who divorced, but still met occasionally to have sex. Obviously, their marriage fell apart because of other factors.

I think we all can agree that a good sex life is necessary if we want to have the best marriage possible, but how do we qualify a good sex life? Can it be measured by frequency? Maybe, but not every time. How active a good sex life is depends on the couple, and it can vary widely. What is a minimum for many couples is a maximum for others, but if compatibility exists, both are right.

I think the key word here is compatibility. An enjoyable, fulfilling sexual experience may only happen once or twice and month for some couples, but it can be once a day for others. If both couples are satisfied with the arrangement, then both have a good-quality sex life.

I'm convinced that a good sex life can smooth out many little wrinkles in a marriage because of the pleasurable experience it brings to both partners. However, let me make something very clear: Sex can only sustain a marriage for so long. If your marriage is based solely on sex, then eventually your relationship is going to come apart. According to a recent study, 40-million Americans have a sexless marriage.

Why? As we age, sexual activity naturally slows down, and although medical science has extended the possibility for a good sex life by decades (for many), it's still a fact that for every marriage, sex will one day be a minor part of that relationship. When that happens you may still have decades of life ahead of you. That's why a balanced life of relationships makes sense. You still can have a satisfying marriage, but one facet—sex—won't be as dominant. But let's get back to sex in a young to middle-aged marriage.

One of the things I've discovered is that the sex drive in individuals varies, and I don't mean just slightly. Everyone is born with a different mix of genes and glands. Of course, in puberty, it may seem that every teenager has a sex engine that's roaring to get started, and all men and women are created equal in sexual terms. However, that's certainly not true.

A minority of men produce a very high level of natural testosterone, and some men maintain that level throughout most of their adult lives. Young males who have this genetic makeup are so driven by the desire to have sex that it's unusual for them to go even 24 hours without having some sort of sexual experience. On the other hand, another minority of males have an extremely low sex drive. It's just the way they were built. To have sex once a week or every other week suits them just fine.

But these are the extremes, and probably only 5 percent of males are in the very high or very low category. Most fall somewhere in-between these extremes.

But let's don't just talk about the male sex drive. Females are endowed with some of the same levels of desire or lack of desire as their male counterparts. Years ago it was assumed only males had a built-in sex drive and females were passive; in fact women who flaunted their sexuality were considered abnormal. However, we've learned that females have a wide range of characteristics when it comes to desire, and the Victorian posture of our great-grandmothers has been replaced by openness and sometimes even an aggressiveness that mimics the most testosterone-enhanced males.

Of course, we all know men and women who fit into the high or low-end categories. We know them because they stand out, either because of their open sexiness or lack of it. I think it's important for adults who are contemplating an ongoing sexual relationship—living together or marriage—to identify a potential life-mate's sexual compatibility. In an extended dating situation, the level of sexual desire present in the two individuals is usually evident. In my opinion, that should be one of the primary reasons for a decent engagement period. A couple should have this time in order to get to know each other in every way possible.

Yes, that's right, and since sex is the primary reason for marriage, knowing a person's sexual drive, or lack of it, is certainly critical to a successful relationship. I'm not advocating premarital sexual activity here, but I am recommending an awareness of your prospective partner's level of sexual desire.

But let me clarify something: It's not critical to exactly peg a prospective mate's level of sexual desire. Most men and women are going to fall somewhere in the broad 80-percent national average, which means they aren't going to be off the wall sexually, or completely absent of sexual desire. You're only going to see true sexual incompatibility with individuals who mistakenly marry someone on the opposite end of the spectrum.

Am I making too much out of sexual compatibility? I don't think so. If we're talking about a potential long-term relationship that begins with one sexually charged individual and another with a mild sexual appetite, then the odds of that marriage having serious problems are huge. Both partners will feel sexual frustration. One will think of the other as a sexual addict, and the other will believe their partner is frigid. A male with an extremely active sex drive, for example, who is married to a woman with a very low sex drive has a marriage that already has one wheel off. I don't think it takes a genius to see conflict almost daily in that marriage, and affairs are almost sure to come. Thank goodness most of us are somewhere in the middle of that equation. Being just slight off-kilter isn't going to ruin a good relationship.

Okay, let's say you're fairly compatible—maybe not completely, but pretty close. What now? Well, there are several basic features that are common to people with a good sex life. The keys to having a mutually satisfying sexual experience boil down to honesty and openness. If there is a bottom line to a good-quality sex life within a marriage, it is transparency. That's right, complete transparency. Unless you can open up and talk about every little aspect of your sexual desires and fantasies, and can be free in your expression with your mate, you're missing out on a completely fulfilling relationship.

I know you might say, "Well, that takes away some of the mystery and intrigue." Maybe. But for every bit of mystery you lose, you gain much more in understanding and intimacy with your partner. By not sharing your deepest thoughts, you're risking not pleasing your partner, or not being pleased by your mate. You may be one of the lucky few who, without ever expressing yourself, have developed the perfect sexual experience. However, it's more likely that you just think you have a good sex life, and, if your partner opened up and was completely honest about everything, you'd be surprised.

Wouldn't it be better to know exactly how your spouse felt about his or her sexual experience? Sure it would, and when a two people can talk freely and openly about sex, there's not anything they can't discuss. That's when marriage moves up a notch in quality

So don't limit your sexual freedom. If you do, you won't fully enjoy the pleasurable recreation available from sexual intercourse.

Well, it may seem a little daunting to become completely intimate with your spouse. For starters, if you've been very Victorian in your sexual ethics, such as sleeping a long nightgown, never undressing in front of your partner, and quietly having sex under the sheets once a week, you're not ready for total immersion into Twenty-First Century sex.

To move into the Twenty-First Century sexually, you should mimic a stripper who takes off one piece of clothing at a time, and slowly begin to break down those long-standing sexual barriers until you move into to a more relaxed atmosphere in your march to total sexual freedom. If you surprised your wife or husband with total sexual freedom—everything at one time—they'd probably think you have a mental condition. So, where do you start?

Let me give you a good place—the marriage bed. First, I'm assuming you sleep in one bed. If you don't sleep together, and there's no physical reason not to, then start immediately. Now let's move to step two. Go into your bedroom and remove the top sheet so you only have the bottom sheet over the mattress. Then, if you have one, put a down comforter on the bed. If you don't have a comforter, go buy one. It will be one of the best investments you'll ever make.

Since almost everyone lives in a climate-controlled house, a down comforter can be used all year. (They make thinner ones if the summer heat gets to be too much.) The next step is to put the down comforter on the bed, and the bed is made.

Then you can start the first part of your march to complete sexual freedom. When you and your spouse retire that night, announce that the bed has been made especially to accommodate sleeping in the nude. Don't take no for an answer, or leave any article of clothing on, no matter how small. The down comforter will hold a uniform temperature, and you'll feel a freedom from clothing you haven't felt before.

Naturally, the sexual opportunities will abound as your two bodies touch. And after you've slept this way for a few weeks, you won't even think about going back to pajamas. Oh, one more thing I failed to mention. If you have a king-sized bed, get rid of it. A queen-sized one will do just fine, and you won't lose your spouse in that big back forty bed. If you haven't guessed by now, I'm promoting togetherness as one key to a great marriage. And by the time you finish this book I hope you'll understand how togetherness will strengthen your marriage.

Yes, I know almost everyone has children, but bedroom doors can be locked and a robe kept by the bed in case a youngster makes a late-night call. Believe me, sleeping nude under a comforter is one of the best ways to increase your closeness, but don't stop there; move on toward total intimacy.

Let's face it, most of the stuff we see on TV and in the movies, which pretends to show intimacy, gives true intimacy a bad name. The intimacy I'm talking about doesn't constitute a vulgar public display of the human body. Pure intimacy is always between two people who are each in love and want to please the other in the most fulfilling way possible. I think everyone who gets married has that as a goal, but for some reason very few couples achieve it. Let's look a possible obstructions which stand in the way of achieving complete intimacy.

First, and probably the most difficult thing to overcome, is the lack of verbal freedom in sexual expression. There seems to be a taboo that somehow prevents us from sexually expressing ourselves to our spouse. We don't seem to have trouble at a ballgame or at a political rally, but after an unsatisfactory sexual experience many couples clam up. However, that unwillingness to express sexual desires or talk about the lack of pleasure during sexual intercourse can easily create a frosty relationship, which translates into a staid relationship. Remember that a failure to communicate is just the tip of the iceberg, which often leads to incompatibility, separation, and even divorce.

Let me give you an example of how verbal freedom works. A beautiful girl walks by a couple at a restaurant and what happens? Well, most men will glance at her, really wanting to get a better look, but afraid their wives will see them gazing at another woman, which will create a problem. The same thing holds true for many women when an attractive man walks by. She's afraid her husband will see her looking at him, so she tries to act as if he didn't exist.

Is this how you build up a relationship of verbal sexual freedom? No, of course not. Do we have a problem here? Yes, we do and here's why. Is there anything wrong with admiring attractive people? Let's take it one step further: What if we're not just looking, but we're sexually fantasizing about that woman or man? Evidently, a lot of couples think that eye-flirting is a problem, because, I guess, they think the spouse is mentally committing adultery. Yes, that's the bottom line. When you really consider that premise, it seems far-fetched. Well, if that's not the reason for being bothered by your spouse looking at an attractive individual, then what is the reason? Of course, there's really not a good reason.

How many arguments have been started when one or the other sees their spouse looking at an attractive person of the opposite sex, and maybe even passing along a smile? I sure can think of more than a few, and from both sides of our marriage. As I think back on our married life, I remember one particular incident that caused a nasty, vocal fight—when we got home.

We'd been married only a few weeks, and we were in college at the University of Arkansas. Well, we scraped up enough money for tickets to a hot movie, and we made the first showing that

Friday night. Good film, but a bad ending—and I don't mean the movie.

When we walked out of the theater, we passed a line of students waiting for the second show to start. There was more eye-flirting and ogling of my good-looking new wife than I could believe, and to top it off, she seemed to enjoy it. When we got in the car I jumped her with, "I can't believe you flirted with all those guys!" Vertis shot back, something about me smiling at some of the co-eds, but back then I was under the mistaken opinion that it was all right for the male to eye and smile, but not a newly married wife. Who was right? Well, guys can be pretty possessive when it comes to their mates, especially if they're newly-weds, but to make a long story short, I was wrong—dead wrong. To understand why I was wrong let's take a look at nature—both human and animal.

All those animal fights between like species—the ones we see on Animal Planet are over one thing, the right to mate. Think about that for a minute. Surely we're not stuck down there with the lions and tigers when it comes to sexual possessiveness—but are we? Was my anger the same as a bull elephant's? Yes, I must admit it was totally my fault that we argued about young guys flirting with my new wife. But was it wrong for Vertis to bask in the attention and actually flirt back? No, she did nothing wrong at all. She was completely innocent. Here's why: First, to be honest, I'd eyed more than one attractive co-ed in the same line; in fact, I actually smiled and winked at a couple. Pretty hypocritical of me to yell at Vertis wasn't it? But let's look at the bottom line. Was there harm done to the marriage? No, of course not. What was the final outcome of the argument? Well, after a short time we made up, and I quickly found out that the flirting had moved our arousal button up quite a bit. The evening ended in a sexual embrace. We both learned something from that little squabble, and how silly it was to be jealous over something as minor as flirtation.

Thankfully, we got over that silliness early in our marriage, but you'd be amazed at how many couples haven't, and it sure isn't a problem just with new marriages. I've seen irrational arguments about flirting come up in 20, 30, or even 40-year-old marriages. So what's the solution? Do we have to condition ourselves to turn our heads when a good-looking person of the opposite sex walks by? And if we get caught looking should we feel guilty? No and no, and this is why. First off, flirting is part of the natural order of things, and whether it's done discreetly or openly, it's just part of life. And let me throw my two-cents-worth in here on flirting: It's one of the small pleasures in life which I enjoy immensely—and, by the way, Vertis feels the same way. But how can you get over this problem. For the first year or so of our marriage both Vertis and I would pounce on the other, if we got caught giving an attractive person of the opposite sex a second glance. However, as our marriage, and especially our sexual conversations, became more and more transparent, we finally realized that not only were we wasting our breath fussing about eye-flirting, but we could use it to add a little spice to our relationship. It didn't come overnight, but we finally reached a point where not only each of us felt free to look at attractive people, and heck, maybe smile or eye-flirt. And when they passed, we'd comment on the person. Vertis might say, "Those aren't real." And I would usually respond, "Oh, I think you're wrong. Mother Nature made some girls more equal than others." And we would both laugh.

We'd continue the conversation in a light-hearted manner as if we were talking about what to order off the menu. That's the measure of sexual intimacy you should strive for, because to be able to converse about being sexually attracted to another member of the opposite sex is stimulating to your partner and will make for a more free expression of sexual desire.

Now let's dig a little deeper into sexuality. Of course, the final measure of sexual intimacy is expressed during sexual intercourse, and that's where the true measure of sexuality must occur. If this act of ultimate intimacy is flawed, then one or both partners will receive less than a full measure of pleasure. It's certainly no secret that every married couple's utmost desire has to do, in part, with a fulfilled sexual relationship, but you'd be surprised how few couples reach their potential. Actually, many couples think they have a good-quality sex life, but don't, because they're limited by the lack of sexual freedom and verbal sexual expression.

Again verbal freedom comes into play, and sometimes it's the freedom to say "some other time," or "that didn't work," or "I don't want to do it that way again." How is your partner going to know he or she isn't pleasing you if you act as if you've taken a vow of silence? And I don't mean the trite comment, "Was it good for you?" If you have to ask, the answer is usually no, but you probably won't hear the word.

Well then, how can a couple achieve the best possible sex? I guess more has been written about that question than about almost anything in marriage. Couples struggle through poor-quality sex thinking their problems are common with every marriage. And often these couples are hesitant to even voice their displeasure to each other, and going to a marriage counselor because full sexual pleasure is not being received is something few couples will do.

Then where do we start? First, couples should have complete sexual intimacy to the point where each person feels free to express to their partner, in graphic terms, exactly what gives them the most pleasure—and if there are parts of the love-making that don't give them pleasure. You'd be surprised how many men and women leave a sexual encounter less than fully satisfied, but you would be even more surprised at how many actually express their frustrations to their spouse.

Often, early in a marriage, sexual encounters are quick and passionate, but newly married couples (with their frequency of intercourse) usually compensate for that problem. However, if intercourse continues over the years to be a quick almost mechanical response to the urge to copulate, one or both partners will soon feel short-changed. Sometimes it's just youth, and there are ways to compensate. But many times, it's the male partner's lack of consideration or understanding that causes the problem. That's when the openness of the relationship comes into play. If you're in a marriage where the male is selfishly just relieving himself, then you need to spell it out in black and white; and if he doesn't change or get some help—a wife might withhold sex until he does. I guarantee that will get his attention!

Married couples have an expression of intimacy, as lovers, which can't be duplicated. That's the sex life each one of us wants to have in our marriage relationship, and, if you have a high quality sex life, it's possible to maintain it for decades—not just when you're young.

I've touched on the mental part of sex, but I haven't given it the emphasis it deserves. When Vertis and I were first married, our arousal was basically an on/off switch. However, as any married couple can attest, when a couple matures and their marriage comes under the stress of work, kids, or the thousand other things that pull at us each day, the on/off button becomes more like a sliding electrical dimmer switch, which only moves in increments toward the arousal stage.

Be very aware of that, or you may mistake the rejection of an offer to have sex as a "no," when it is actually it's a "not now." And believe it or not, the "not now" may actually mean "yes, but in a few minutes."

Consider the following: You've had a relative easy day at work and late in the afternoon, with nothing else to do, you fanaticize about having sex with your spouse. When you come home, you're ready for immediate gratification, but you are met with, "Now? You've got to be kidding? After the day I've had?"

It surprised you. It shouldn't have.

Your spouse's day could easily have been one packed with stress and work. A sliding switch replaced his or her on/off button years ago, and it sure wasn't anywhere close to being up at the arousal level after a rough day. So, what's the solution? First, the marriage partners must be fully aware of the mental aspects of sex. Unless you are, solving the arousal problem will be difficult. But let's assume you do understand how mental sex really is. If we can make that a starting point, then here's how to move the sliding switch up to the arousal level.

But first let's discuss how the mental part of sex changes as your marriage ages. Vertis and I had been married less than two years when I took a transfer to Benghazi, Libya. There, I worked for Esso Libya as a well-site geologist, supervising the evaluation of exploratory oil wells drilled in the Libyan Desert. We had a mountain of college debt and the pay was double what I was making in the states, so we took the transfer.

What has that got to do with sex—mentally? Well, let me explain the job, and I think you'll understand. On a typical Monday morning, I'd go out to the Benghazi airport and get on a single engine plane called a Beaver. We'd fly about two hours into the desert, landing beside a drilling rig where I'd spend two or three weeks evaluating the rocks we drilled through—to determine if any oil or gas was present. That was the easy part. Staying out in the desert without going back to Benghazi and my new bride was the hard part.

Picture this: You have two young, newly married, highly sexual individuals, who have been separated for two or three weeks, who love each other very much and have counted the days apart. Vertis would meet me at the airport, we'd have a passionate kiss, and then jump in the car and head for our villa. When we arrived, guess how much foreplay we had before having sex? Well, if you guessed over a minute, you were too high. We'd park the car, not even get my bags out, run into the house, and as soon as the door closed behind us begin shedding clothes. We would jump into bed and began having sex immediately. (The first time was pretty brief, as you might guess.)

That's an example of the on/off switch of sexual arousal. However, let's fast forward about 40 years. Now, instead of rushing sex, we take our time. Maybe some extra touching that morning even before we get out of bed, and then, before I leave for work, we'll turn up the affection level. Maybe one of us will even say our key phrase, "How about a date later?"

During the day we'll continue the anticipation by reminding each other about our upcoming date. Just little things, but believe me it's the little things that began to move the arousal switch. At lunch it might be an extra kiss a caress, or a suggestive comment. Anything to keep our minds moving toward the time when we can sexually express ourselves.

Every couple works out a time when they can have sexual intercourse. Our most frequent time is around six in the evening—a time we settled on after our kids went off to college. A typical summer date might start with a skinny dip in our swimming pool, complete with lots of tender touching. Sometimes that leads directly into sex, but not usually. After our swim, we move to the bedroom, sip some wine, talk, and listen to some jazz. I know this seems involved and might seem to be taking an inordinate amount of time and effort. However, in our marriage, it clears our minds and moves our arousal switches to the place where we can get serious about having sex.

Occasionally, even after all that preparation and extended foreplay, it doesn't work. And if that happens, one of us will end it by saying simply, "It's not working." The other will usually agree and we'll stop. However, most of the time foreplay turns our arousal switches fully on, and we have a successful sexual experience.

Before we leave the subject of planning a special "date," I want to make one thing very clear: It's fine to plan ahead to have sex, but don't make every sexual encounter a planned event. I've had times when Vertis was undressing, and I happened to walk in the room. A touch, caress—maybe a kiss—and the urge hits us. The rule for sex is that there are no rules. Mix it up, but keep this in mind: When you feel tired and overworked and not in the mood to have sex, admit it and wait. Guys, don't let the macho man in you keep you from saying, "Later." Nothing in this situation is worse than a pathetic attempt to make love. There is a time to simply say, "It's not working."

Now, let's discuss the infrequent times we use that phrase. Over the years we've had occasional spells where, for one reason or another, our attempts to have sex flopped. The first few times it happened we were devastated. However, as we matured, so did our understanding. Now, and for quite a number of years, if that happens, we can even laugh about it. It's no big deal, and we know that the little mental problems we couldn't shake will be gone the next time we try. That's important, because to blame one or the other for this kind of failure can lead to some deep-seated sexual problems, and put unbelievable pressure on a couple the next time they try to have sex. (Believe me, there're very few men who can't point to times of impotency.)

Another key to sexual intimacy is linked together mentally and physically. This important relationship item is just about the simplest you can imagine. It's the act of touching. No, I don't mean foreplay before intercourse, which, of course, should happen as a natural part of sex. I'm talking about an attitude of touching, starting with that first cup of coffee in the morning and ending with a snuggle at the end of a long day. There's something physiologically stimulating about just the touch of a hand. Physiologists have noted that almost every time you touch your mate, it is an automatic sexual stimulus. Of course, moving an affection level up doesn't always lead to sex, but it does act as a stimulus to increase the chances for future successful sexual encounters.

Flirting moves up to a different level with a touch, and married couples who caress reinforce intimacy every time they touch. A marriage without touching is usually one that is riddled with sexual problems. It's an unnatural act for two individuals who haven't as much as touched during the day to grasp each other sexually; it's awkward, and the attempted intercourse is probably brief and unfulfilling.

So try this: rubs on the shoulder over coffee, a touch on the cheek, and an open- mouth kiss sometime before separation for work. Maybe after work, find a secluded spot and caress your partner in an intimate spot—but make this playful, flirty, and sexual, all at the same time.

Each touch should be a reminder to your partner that you desire him or her.. Touching is an invitation to more intimacy, and each touch builds upon the last. I think touching is so important, in fact, that later in this book I have amplified this section into an entire chapter.

And last, but certainly not least, the sex act is a partnership. That's right. It's not a situation where one gives and the other takes. Only when a couple understands that the need for sexual fulfillment is as important to one as it is to the other will that couple have a good sex life.

A number of years back, I had a young, very attractive woman confide to me that her husband seemed to never consider her when they made love. Their problems were a lot more complicated than his premature ejaculation—which she thought was keeping her from being satisfied. No, that was the symptom, but the problems in their marriage ran much deeper. Her husband, while not admitting it, considered sexual intercourse to be a selfish act, only for the male's enjoyment.

Nothing could be further from the truth. If your sexual partner isn't usually achieving the same level of sexual satisfaction you are, then you have sexual problems in your marriage, and believe me, these problems can cause even a good marriage to founder. It did for this young woman. As a sidelight to her story, she divorced and remarried a man who fit her exactly, sexually. They have one of the best marriages I know of.

I'd be leaving out a part of the sexual experience if I didn't cover items that enhance the act. The mechanical, rubber, or silicone sex toys are readily available, but should they be used? Sure, they should, if the couple agrees. Let's face it folks, sex with the same man or woman can always use some spice after years and years of the same thing.

If you can add something that excites both participants and makes the experience more enjoyable, I can't imagine why you wouldn't. There are such a wide variety of items I couldn't possibly cover them is this manual. My advice is to buy some and give them a try. I guarantee you two things: If as a couple you agree to give them a try and keep an open mind, you may increase the excitement of your sexual experiences.

A final comment about sex toys: Don't use them every time, and guys—especially guys—don't feel threatened if your wife seems to get more sexual pleasure from one of the toys than she does from you. After all, creating pleasure by having sex is what sexual intercourse is all about. The methods may vary, but the result must always be to bring pleasure to both.

And, finally, what around the chemical enhancements? First, let's talk about drugs designed with the female in mind. As a little background, let me refresh your memory. As females age, a drop in natural hormone levels creates a change of life called menopause. Many times, menopause causes a loss of sexual desire and sometimes it signals the end to a woman's sexual pleasure. It can be frustrating to the husband, but even more upsetting to the woman.

Modern medicine has worked on this problem for a generation, and the result is a regimen of hormone replacement that attempts to replace the loss of female hormones. The two most widely used are Premarin or Prempro, which is conjugated equine estrogens or synthetic progesterone/progestin. The other hormone therapy is called BHRT or bioidentical hormones such as estradiol, a natural human estrogen, and Prometrium, which is bioidentical progesterone. Both attempt to do the same thing by replacing the loss of natural hormones in a woman's body.

After menopause, when a woman's hormone level is low, her vagina can become dry, and sex can be painful. Not only is it painful, but many times the low hormones levels reduce the woman's desire and the sex act itself is no longer pleasurable or fulfilling. (Of course, numerous other problems are tied to low hormones levels, such as osteoporosis. That's one reason why so many women undergo hormone replacement therapy.)

When hormones are taken, many, if not all, the symptoms of menopause disappear and sexual desire returns. Well, it would seem that this treatment would be universally accepted, but that's not the case. Several studies have shown a possible increase in breast cancer in women who take hormones, along with several other side effects. These hormones are like so many of our modern drugs. Almost all of them have both positives and negatives. In other words they all have side effects.

For many common drugs that lower cholesterol, the drug companies list side effects that take several paragraphs to outline. However, people continue to take these drugs because the benefits—in their opinion—outweigh the drawbacks. That's the case for hormone replacement. Each woman should make a calculated and informed decision about whether hormone replacement therapy is right for her.

My premise in writing this book is to tell you what works in my own marriage, and let you decide if those positive features would translate into giving you a more fulfilling marriage, too. Hormone replacement, BHRT, bioidentical hormone therapy, has been a very positive part of our marriage from the first time Vertis started the treatment. She made the choice that the positives outweighed the negatives, and when she began to go through menopause, she decided to begin hormone replacement.

Vertis chose the bioidnetical therapy and it completely eliminated her menopausal symptoms and restored her desire for sex. (Read Suzanne Somers's about hormones to get a better understanding of your options.) Vertis will emphatically tell you that hormone replacement therapy has been an extremely positive part of her middle-aged life. Before Vertis started receiving BHRT pellets—that are surgically inserted as small, time-released tablets—she was in the middle of menopause, having hot flashes. And our sex life, which had been vigorous, was struggling. We were still intimate, but it wasn't the same.

After looking into the various ways to combat menopause, she decided to seek the advice of a Dallas physician. After a consultation, she decided to try the compounded BHRT pellets. That was more than 20-years ago, and Vertis has been on bioidentical hormones ever since. Over the years, she has had numerous mammograms, CT Scans, and yearly physicals. There have been no problems. Vertis also has regular blood work done, so her doctor can be sure the pellets are giving her the right dosage.

Let me give you a spouse's take on her hormone treatment. A week after she had the first bioidentical pellets inserted, we went to Jefferson, Texas, to spend the night in a bed and breakfast—just getting away for a day to rest up from a busy week. Late that afternoon, before dinner, we were in the room leaning back on the bed having a glass of wine. Causal touching led to a kiss. I know my wife and I can sense when she is aroused. This was one of those times, but since she'd been going through menopause the past few months, I hadn't felt that interest from her in quite a while. A few minutes later we were nude in bed caressing each other.

The difference was striking. We made love like we hadn't in a long time and for the first time in months, she thoroughly enjoyed it. Later that night we had a candlelight dinner. She was excited, and I was beside myself. I had the sexual woman back that I thought I'd lost to menopause. That's my story about hormones.

I have one other thing to say about menopause before I get to the guys. There are many books that detail the pros and cons of ingesting hormones. One of Vertis's favorites is Suzanne Somers' book Ageless: The Naked Truth About Bioidentical Hormones. Hormones may not fit you because of many factors, but if Vertis's experience is typical, then they're worth every penny.

All right, we touched on the ladies, now let's talk about men. Men go through some of the same changes in their bodies as women do. Sometimes they don't have the outward symptoms, but the changes are there. At 45, I bought a bright red XKE Jaguar sports car. Yes, my mid-life crisis was changing not only my body but my mind.

As I aged, it became evident that at 50 or 60 my body wasn't the same as it had been in my 20s or 30s. To compound that, at 38 I'd started to play singles tennis—sometimes as many as five sets a day, four times a week. At 55, I was ranked number one in my age bracket in Arkansas. Tennis helped me stay physically fit, but it did nothing for my sex life, especially after a grueling match in Arkansas's heat and humidity. In fact, after four sets of tennis, having sex was difficult. I started by carefully scheduling our sexual activities on the days when I wasn't playing.

But there are more ways than conserving your strength to keep your sex life active. Thanks to the myriad of new erectile dysfunction drugs it's relatively easy to extend an active sex life well into your 80s And since we're talking about drugs to make a man function, let's dig a little deeper. When drugs such Cialis and Viagra came out they were immediately purchased by men with ED problems. However, soon these drugs moved down the age bracket, and now they are commonly purchased by college kids to be sure they can perform on a "hot" date.

Are these drugs something that most men should consider using? I think so. But be careful, since these drugs can react to other drugs you may be taking, and that can cause serious side effects. As the drug makers say, "First ask your doctor if you're in shape to have sexual intercourse".

But let's say you're like a lot of men maybe in your 40s or 50s and you don't have erectile dysfunction, but you're not the man sexually you were in your 20s—actually no one is. As your testosterone dropped over the years, your sex drive was affected. The firm erection you had 10 years ago isn't there anymore, and you frequently have trouble maintaining it during intercourse. Of course, it might not be testosterone. It could be many things. But let's say you are physically in decent shape, and are still able to have sex. Are you a candidate for these drugs? In my opinion; of course you are. If by taking a chemical enhancement, with limited side effects, that will improve your sex life, why wouldn't you do it?

Let me give you a personal example. When these drugs first came out I would have been embarrassed to ask my doctor to give me a prescription, as would most men. However, as the drugs became more widely used, I realized they just might help my performance. I've had very few problems with impotence, but, as with most men, occasionally it did happen. On vacation, it was rare, and the frequency of intercourse then would easily double the activity when we were home.

What made me a believer was attempting to have sex in the late afternoon, after a long day of when work problems that had put me under stress. When late in the afternoon came around, and it was a time for us to disrobe, have a glass of wine, and relax in the bed, it was hard for me to get sex on my mind.

Sometimes we would try and create some excitement by talking sexy, kissing or touching, but we still had problems "getting in the mood." Let me translate that: Sometimes I couldn't get a good erection. Listen, fellows, when that happens, throw in the towel because the resulting experience won't be of the quality you're used to, and your wife will know it. And, by the way, if you have total transparency in your sex life, it won't be a traumatic experience; it will just be recognizing that the time isn't right for sex.

Well, after a few of those times, I started taking ¼ of a Viagra pill. (Now I take 1/2 of a Cialis.) Believe me, it made a difference.

It's the same principal as a college kid on a hot date—it's like buying an insurance policy. Just making sure you're ready and able when the time is right. Look at it this way: All men, as they age, will come to a time when they can't have sex easily without chemical enhancement. It's usually not one day they can and the next they can't. It's a subtle change that takes place over several years. You might still be able to perform, but you aren't the same as you were a few years back.

Let me explain. The mechanism that gives a man an erection is just like any part of your body. If you're 50, your heart doesn't function as efficiently as it did when you were 20, and that goes for your sexual organ, too. These drugs not only help you achieve an erection, but they make an ordinary erection at age 50 or 60 extra-ordinary.

A couple will receive more pleasure and satisfaction from this experience—by far—than they would if the male had an incomplete erection.

This book will not cover all the possibilities that are out there on the market. Some doctors are offering testosterone implants and human growth hormones to mask the effect of sexual aging. Do they work? According to many men, they do. However, these particular drugs have many more side effects than the common erectile dysfunction drugs. (More on this subject in a later chapter.)

***

But there may be more than just a pleasure to be gained from frequent sexual intercourse. In his book on male sexual health, The Hardness Factor, Dr. Steven Lamm cites a British study in which men who reported having three or more orgasms per week experienced 50 percent fewer heart attacks and strokes, compared with those who had less frequent orgasms. Lamm's book was inspired by the correlations he made in his own practice between the diminished erectile quality of his male patients and conditions like obesity, high cholesterol, hypertension, depression, sleep disorders, diabetes, and heart disease.

According to Lamm, "On the surface, it looks as though the principal message of this study is that having sex reduces the incidence of heart attack and stroke and lets you live longer..."

And there's more evidence of the sex–health link: A recent study published in the "Journal of the American College of Cardiology" reported that erectile dysfunction is often an early indicator of poor cardiovascular health. Researchers followed some 2,300 men for an average of four years and found that men with ED had a 58 percent greater risk of coronary heart disease.

Sex researcher Stuart Brody writes in the "Journal of Sexual Medicine" that a cause-and-effect relationship exists between sex and better health. While the underlying reasons for these health improvements might be unclear, here's a list of health benefits apparently enjoyed by many people who have frequent sex.

1. A longer life

In a British study, men who had intercourse at least twice a week lived longer than men who had sex less than once a month. A U.S. study reported similar findings, and a Swedish study examining the sex lives of 70-year-olds found that men who died before their 75th birthday had ceased having sexual intercourse at earlier ages.

The Swedish study did not find that women lived longer if they had sex more often, and neither did a study in North Carolina. However, in the North Carolina study, women who reported enjoying sex more lived longer than those who didn't report enjoyment.

2. A healthier heart

In a British study, people who had intercourse twice a week or more were less likely to suffer heart attacks and other fatal coronary events. Those who had sex less than once a month had twice the rates of fatal coronary events, compared to those with the highest frequency of intercourse.

3. Lower blood pressure

In a study published in the "Journal of Biological Psychology," people who had sex more often tended to have lower diastolic blood pressure—the bottom number in a blood pressure reading. Stuart Brody's experiment, in which more sexually active study subjects had markedly less dramatic blood pressure spikes when they were put under stress, also supports the benefit.

4. Lower risk of breast cancer

A French study found that women who had vaginal intercourse not at all, or infrequently, had three times the risk of breast cancer, compared with women who had intercourse more often.

5. Lower risk of prostate cancer

A Minnesota study found that men who'd had intercourse more than 3,000 times in their lives had half the prostate cancer risk of those who had not. While it's not clear why this would be true, studies have found that men who had more intercourse tended to have better prostate function and eliminated more waste products in their semen. "These differences could conceivably impact prostate cancer risk," Brody wrote.

6. Pain relief

Whipple and others have conducted studies suggesting that more sexual activity helps relieve lower back pain and migraines.

7. A slimmer physique

A study of healthy German adults revealed that men and women who had sex more frequently tended to be slimmer than folks who didn't have as much sex. Sex burns 50-to-60 calories per encounter, Whipple says, so sex three times a week for a month would burn some 700 calories—or the equivalent of jogging about seven miles.

8. Better testosterone levels

A group of men being treated for erectile problems saw greater increases in testosterone when, along with the treatments, they had frequent sex. Specifically, men who had sex at least eight times per month had greater increases than those who had sex fewer than eight times per month.

9. Fewer menopause symptoms

Menopausal women in Nigeria reportedly experienced fewer hot flashes when they had sex more frequently. This may be because sexual activity helps regulate hormonal levels, which in turn affect the symptoms of menopause, reported Brody.

10. Healthier semen

In three studies, men who had frequent intercourse had a higher volume of semen, a higher sperm count and a higher percentage of healthier sperm, compared with men who tended to participate in other sexual activities.

***

Well, to sum it up. What should be the sexual goal for a committed couple trying to achieve a top-quality life? Very simply put, the goal should be to maintain a high quality sex life for as long as possible. If drugs, exercise, or something else can help, we should utilize any legal means to enjoy a positive sexual marriage relationship.

As I finish this chapter, I would like to add a word for those of you with marriage problems who are not having a good-quality sex life. It may be that your marriage rough spots are directly related to your sex problems. If you think that's the case, then swallow your shyness and get professional help. But whatever you do, don't ignore these problems. If you do, they will invariable lead to affairs or divorce, and will certainly reduce the intimacy in your marriage.

As I said earlier in this chapter, a satisfying, pleasurable sexual experience with your mate is a prerequisite if you're going to reach the 95th percentile and live the best life possible.

Premise # 5

You must be fit to have a top-quality marriage, and live the best life possible

You Must Be Physically Fit

A physically fit couple, living a healthy lifestyle, has a much better chance to have a top-quality marriage, than an unfit couple living an unhealthy lifestyle. That's a simple straightforward statement, and nothing could be truer. However, since most couples are usually in fairly good shape when they marry, being fit and living a healthy lifestyle may not be a high priority, especially to the young who feel bulletproof. Yes, these young couples may have a great marriage for a few blissful years, but I'm not writing about surviving marriage and living the best life possible just for those first few heady years. I want you to have a superior marriage, one that's an ultimate relationship, which will last for decades.

This chapter will focus on not only what we can do to reach that quality marriage level we're all trying to achieve, but what can we do to extend it. Your goal should be to achieve a top-quality marriage as soon as possible, and keep it for as long as possible, in order to live the best life possible. But you can't do that unless you're physically fit.

Obviously, instead of trying to build and maintain a healthy, fit lifestyle, a newlywed couple can just plod along decade after decade and ignore the fitness and lifestyle part of their relationship. Actually, according to government surveys, some 63 percent of the population is either overweight or obese. So it's obvious a majority of Americans do just that—ignore living a healthy lifestyle. There may be some fit and healthy folks in that 63 percent but not very many. Being overweight and fit just don't go together. Look at it this way: Just by being fit you can automatically move the quality of your marriage up above average. And the bottom line, as far as I'm concerned, is that a fit couple is well on their way to a top-quality marriage.

Many Americans have a short-term outlook on health and fitness. Most of the obese or even the overweight people you talk with aren't satisfied with their level of fitness, and they will usually mention a diet they're about to go on, or a health club they're about to join. But the facts are conclusive: many of these otherwise healthy adults won't do much about their fitness. They'll make half-hearted attempts to diet or join a health club for a few weeks, and every year their New Year's resolutions will have to do with diet and fitness. But they rarely follow through, and, as they procrastinate, the unhealthy lifestyle will catch up with them. One penalty for being unfit can be a gradual degrading, or maybe an abrupt end, to their once- good marriage. One day their marriage, and their life, will only be a shadow of what it was or could be.

When you examine the consequences of living for the present and ignoring the physical side of life, the negatives will shock you. Yes, for every action, or in this case inaction, there is a consequence, and sometimes those consequences are severe. Millions of married couples, just in the United States, have less than a good-quality marriage because one or both of the individuals are unfit or living an unhealthy lifestyle. These couples can't possibly be in the 95th percentile.

So, how should newlyweds begin married life? It's as simple as good common sense. They should set realistic, long-term goals for their marriage, and all of those goals should have one thing in common: They should work to ensure that their actions will result in positive consequences, not negative, and that the marriage and lifestyle goals will continually enhance their life.

Naturally, almost every couple would agree with the above statement, but you'd be amazed at the number of marriages where at least one of the partners is unfit. Good intentions—if not followed through—won't make you fit or improve your life. Being fit and living a healthy lifestyle is such an obvious part of a good-quality marriage that you would think it would be one of the most important items in every marriage. But sadly it isn't.

Before I discuss the details of being fit and living healthy lifestyle, I want to discuss the idea of togetherness in fitness. I believe, if you are to live a top-quality life, both of the marriage partners must be equally fit. Unless that's the case, sooner or later, that marriage will be one of an unequally yoked couple—physically—and marriage problems will loom. Just consider that premise for a second. An unfit partner eventually won't be able to participate in many normal physical activities. And, as the marriage matures, there will come a point when the unfit partner will essentially drop out. They might not die, but they will no longer substantially contribute to the marriage. For all practical purposes, the marriage is over, and their dream to live the best life possible will have disappeared.

The basic reason to seek fitness together has to do with consistency and encouragement. When a couple works out together, they'll encourage each other and the consistency of the workout will always be better. Look at it this way: If only one of the marriage partners is fit, the unfit partner may push his or her spouse to miss workouts.

In our marriage it works exactly in that manner. Vertis actually began working out before I did and encouraged me to start. Today we are at the workout center before 6 a.m. most mornings to get our aerobic workout, and in the afternoon, while she is doing Pilates, I get my weight work done. Believe me, marriage partners who work out together have a much better chance of maintaining a healthy lifestyle than those who don't.

But back to getting started early in your marriage: In our 20s and 30s we think we're made of steel. Our sexual activity soars, and we feel on top of the world. Ahhaa, if we could only stay that age forever, but Father Time won't let us. Soon those couples who blew through the early years of their marriage find themselves facing middle age, and before they know it, old age creeps up on them, and soon they're facing the later years of their life.

Many young couples act as if old age will never overtake them, and when it sneaks up on them and gradually drags them into inactivity, they act as if it's a surprise. When that happens, what had been a good-quality marriage, and life, is lost forever. The couple may live for another 30 years, but they won't be living a top-quality life. They have lost decades of their once-great marriage—and that loss was self-inflicted. They will find themselves on the prayer list at the church, and they'll have no one to blame but themselves.

Since the goal in this book is to not only survive marriage, but to make it the ultimate relationship where you have the opportunity to live the best life possible, it makes sense that we'd want it to last as long as possible. But it's not just longevity we're talking about: It's quality. After we pass 50, it becomes harder and harder to participate in activities we once took for granted. But if we want to be active in our later years, we can't wait until we're 50 or 60 to try and get in shape. What we do in our 20s and 30s will go a long way in shaping our late- life fitness.

I'm not saying, that if you haven't worked out and you're 60 years old it's too late. No, you can still recover and extend you optimum lifestyle, but it won't ever come up to the level you could have achieved if you had started during the early years of your marriage. The earlier a couple begins regular fitness training, the better the outlook.

I guess everything should have a bottom line of importance, and for me it's the fact, that, unless you're physically fit, your sex life will go downhill in a hurry after 60, especially if you're a smoker. However, studies have shown this dire expectation can be put off for decades—if a man is physically fit, has never smoked, and possibly has a good supply of Cialis, Levitra, or Viagra.

Yes, as you know from the last chapter, I, personally believe in taking legal, sexual performance enhancing drugs. Actually, a number of studies indicate that these drugs, especially Levitra or generic Vardenafil, can be very effective in treating or preventing COPD (Chronic Obstructive Pulmonary Disease). These drugs also treat Metabolic Syndrome and premature ejaculation, and there are some indications that they reduce inflammation in the some heart arteries. Those are what you might call positive side-effects.

Well, extending your sex life is great, but of course there are many other reasons to stay fit. A fit marriage partner is one who can easily participate and get involved in physical activities that build up common interests and expend kinetic energy. More and more older adults are joining in activities that their grandparents would find hard to believe. By participating in these activities with your marriage partner, you will be continually building your marriage instead of seeing it slowly deteriorate—and your high quality of life will be extended for decades.

The idea behind anything we do in marriage, especially when it comes to fitness, should be to enhance our relationship, and when we reach the plateau of a good-quality marriage, extend it for as long as possible. If that means playing mixed doubles tennis into our 80s, or being involved in Senior Olympics because we're fit, that's great! It all boils down to living an enhanced, top-quality life for as long as possible—and enjoying it together.

Fitness is no different than any other lifestyle component. Everything you do should be evaluated. Does it promotes a good-quality life or take away from one? If you've paid any attention to this book it should be obvious by now that there are positives and negatives in all marriage relationships. My goal is to remove as many of the negatives from your marriage as possible and replace them with positives.

Think of it this way: You smoke, and you know it's a big negative. Let's evaluate that negative for a few minutes. Smokers will tell you that when they smoke, it's pleasurable. But they should weigh the positive response they get from smoking against the negative impact upon their body and, ultimately, on their marriage. I can list all of the smoking negatives, but you know them. To sum them up in one sentence is easy. Smoking will shorten a good-quality marriage by several decades. If you smoke, you can't possibly be fit or maintain sexual potency after 60. And as you accumulate all the minuses from decades of smoking it's easy to arrive at this conclusion: "If I smoke, I give up at least 20 years of a top-quality marriage." You have minutes of pleasure each day as a trade-off to losing 20 good years of marriage. Only a fool would continue smoking faced with those consequences.

However, all of the choices we make that affect a good-quality marriage aren't as cut and dried as smoking. It's the small, subtle, personal habits that are hard to give up because we don't see their effects in giant letters written in the sky. As an example, let's examine one seemingly innocent pastime. A friend of mine kept in fair shape, didn't smoke, and, overall, had a healthy lifestyle. But strangely enough he developed arterial blockage at a relatively early age. His doctor looked at his family history, which gave him the first clue. But when he looked closely at my friend's diet—there was the red flag. During the day his diet was so-so— nothing out of the ordinary. And the changes the doctor ordered to lower cholesterol were minor. However, after a closer study of this man's diet, the dietitian spotted the big problem—his bedtime snack. Every night he'd dip up a large bowl of creamy vanilla ice cream, lean back in bed and watch the 10 o'clock news while he devoured it.

Now we all know an occasional bowl of ice cream isn't going to make much difference in your overall health, but a big bowl a day can add up to an astounding 950,000 artery-clogging calories a year, send your cholesterol skyrocketing, and, as it did with my friend, cause heart damage.

Vertis and I love to have an occasional martini before dinner while we talk and listen to jazz. However, we limit ourselves to one a week. If we had one every night it would have a negative impact on the quality of our marriage—and our health. I believe that's the key when you evaluate your lifestyle. Again, it's moderation. I'm a firm believer in enjoying as many of life's pleasures as humanly possible, but when I do, I consider every possible side effect, so I can judge if those activities will have a long-term negative effect on my fitness.

I think, if we're honest in our evaluating our health and look closely at our lifestyle, we can see that many times it's a trade-off. The man or woman who works out frequently can trade-off a workout for an extra drink—occasionally—but, on the other hand, if they have nothing to trade-off, every negative will add to the loss of fitness. A fit body is much more able to withstand the effects of alcohol, for example, than one which is unfit. The fit body's kidneys, liver, and digestive system are stronger and better able to process the alcohol from an occasional drink than an unfit body.

But let's get back to the original premise and focus on fitness and marriage. I know you're wondering if it's really that important to be in shape when you're striving to have a top-quality marriage. In fact, I'm sure you can cite several marriages that have failed because of excessive exercising and others that seem to be clicking along quite nicely as two otherwise healthy people smile and waddle their way through life.

First, let's consider excessive training: It's true that individuals who engage in what I call compulsive over-training, linked to overly competitive events, can weaken and destroy their marriage. These marriage partners have violated two marriage principals: Time and Energy, which we'll address later in this chapter.

But, before you decide I'm negative about strenuous exercise, let me clear things up: I play singles tennis several times a week. Well, that's not so tough in south Arkansas with the mild winters we have, but try it in mid-August with "100 and 100" —that's 100 degrees temperature and 100 percent humidity.

Yes, I believe there's a place for strenuous exercise, but it must be balanced. I don't play tennis in the heat more than twice a week and usually it's only for an hour and a half. I rest and let my body recuperate for a day or two before I go back on the court. But that's not the way the workout kings and queens operate. Many times they work out twice a day for as much as two hours a session.

Is that much exercise beneficial? No, it's not! The simple fact of the matter is that we all have a certain amount of energy. Being fit can increase our energy levels, but only up to a certain point. The person who is obsessive about exercise will eventually have not only physical problems, as his or her body wears out from too much stress, but mental and emotional problems, as well. After all, it's all a matter of energy in and energy out.

Even the fittest of the fit reach their limit when they push themselves. The consequences of over-exercising can impact a marriage as severely as any obsessive habit. When too much energy is expended on physical activity, there may be a shortfall when an opportunity for intimacy presents itself. Sooner or later it's guaranteed to happen. Sometimes one or both of the marriage partners will be just too tired to function. (Many times it's more of a mental tiredness that comes from too much exertion.) Vertis and I work out at least five times a week, and right after a strenuous workout the natural tendency is to rest—not engage in a vigorous sex. We're very open about our sexual needs. The days that I know we have a date planned, I skip any afternoon workouts, or tennis. I can tell you from experience that being fresh when you plan to make love is important. After all, don't we all want a sexual experience to be the best possible? Sure we do.

But back to over-training. We all know individuals who over-train, and if we knew the details of their private lives, I'm sure, just as they have breakdowns of their body parts from excessive training, they have emotional breakdowns, as well. And their sexual dysfunctions become more and more frequent. So don't be an exercise freak—it'll degrade the quality of your marriage.

Now, let's discuss the couple who could be fit and healthy but are waddling their way through life. They may do fine for a few years, but surviving marriage means "till death do us part." Not the first five easy years, but every year until one of the partners dies. This couple represents the millions of marriages where fitness isn't a part of their regular marriage routine. They are the norm, not the exception, it's sad to say. Millions of marriages are not living up to their potential because one or both of the marriage partners are living an unhealthy lifestyle.

If you look at a cross-section of the population, it's obvious that a lot of marriages have one or both marriage partners who aren't in shape. In fact, in a recent release by the U.S. government,

34 percent of the population was found to be not only overweight but obese.

If you don't believe me, spend a few hours watching people in the Atlanta airport. Now Georgia folks don't get upset. All those heavies aren't from Georgia—although a bunch are. By watching people walk down an airport concourse, it's easy to pick out the hundreds upon hundreds of individuals who don't get any on any significant amount of exercise. Take a close look and imagine them making love. Then visualize them making love at 70! Hard to imagine isn't it? Well, it is hard to imagine, because it'll be impossible. I can guarantee you one thing: If they stay in that condition, they'll never reach the quality of marriage that a fit couple will have. Be in the 95th percentile? No, it's impossible.

A recent article from the CNN Health website offered several additional reasons for being fit and not overweight. They quote Ginny Graves from Health.com about the health problems in women who are more than 20 pounds overweight.

Quote: "It's shocking, but it's true. Being a woman who's more than twenty- pounds overweight may actually hike your risk of getting poor medical treatment. In fact, weighing too much can have surprising—and devastating—health repercussions beyond the usual diabetes and heart-health concerns you've heard about for years."

A summary of a few of the findings:

•May have a harder time getting health insurance or have to pay higher premiums.

•Are at higher risk of being misdiagnosed or receiving inaccurate dosages of drugs.

•Are less likely to find a fertility doctor to help with pregnancy..

•Are less likely to have cancer detected early and get effective treatment.

• Typically need more radiation for CT scans than normal weight patients, making it riskier, especially if numerous CT scans are required.

Being overweight can get in the way of effective cancer treatment, too, experts say. The problem is under-dosing. "Oncologists usually base chemo on patients' ideal weight rather than their true weight, partly because chemo is so toxic and partly because drug trials typically include only average women, so we don't know the correct dose for bigger women," says Dr. Kellie Schneider, M. D, a gynecologic oncologist at the University of Alabama at Birmingham.

Studies have also found that overweight women are more likely to delay doctors' appointments and skip preventative care, including screenings for cancer, because they don't want to face criticism.

"It can be frustrating to treat obese patients," admits Dr. Lee Green, M. D. M. P. H., a professor of family medicine at the University of Michigan in Ann Arbor. "I spend most of my time treating the consequences of unhealthy lifestyles instead of actual illnesses. People come in complaining of a foot or knee pain, and I'm thinking, 'Do you not see that you're in pain because you're 60 pounds overweight'? I don't say that of course. I try to encourage them to lose weight."

And from Health.com. "...Compared with women of normal weight (BMI between 22.5 and 25), overweight women were 13 percent more likely to die during the study period. Moderately obese (BMI 30 to 34) and severely obese (BMI 35 to 39) women were 44 percent and 88 percent more likely to die, respectively, while morbidly obese women (BMI 40+) were 2.5 times more likely to die. The pattern was similar for men."

***

I think part of the reason for the lack of fitness in this country is as simple as being young. That's right. Our kids grow up on junk food and our parents and schools don't do enough to change their bad dietary habits. And of course, many young adults from 15 to 25 generally ignore a healthy lifestyle. They smoke–knowing that smoking causes a long list of deadly diseases. They ride motorcycles without a helmets, knowing that one bad turn can make them a vegetable. And because they are sexually active without any physical restraints, they think they'll always be that way. They couldn't be more wrong, because the lifestyle habits they develop in the early years of their marriage are going to be with them until they die—unless they commit to a drastic lifestyle change.

To get a better understanding of why couples should be physically fit, let's look at why not being fit will take away from a quality marriage. Naturally, at a minimum, you reduce the length of your marriage drastically. But it's a lot more than just ending life early. Many of the ways we enjoy marriage are directly tied to being healthy. An unfit marriage partner in their 20s may be able to be involved in most of the activities of a fit partner, and while they can do these things they put fitness out of their mind. What a shortsighted way to look at marriage.

My purpose in writing this book was to help marriage partners reach a level of contentment and pleasure that can be extended for 50 to 60 years, with quality being the criterion. Quality of life—or rather "quality of a marriage"—is the key. As a couple ages, an unfit marriage partner will drop out of many simple activities. Over the course of several decades, what was once a thriving, active marriage will degrade until, for all practical purposes, it's gone.

If you don't stay fit, your physical body will deteriorate much faster than someone who stays fit. I know everyone's body physically deteriorates as we get older, but we've all seen 30-year-olds who are in worse shape than many 60-year-olds. The definition of becoming physically aged really means this: Doing simple things that require a bit of stamina—things you breezed through in your 20s—become an impossible task as you age. When that happens you're old, no matter what your actual age. Your true body age is not determined by your chronological age, it's by your real physical fitness age. It's called your real age, (There is a Real Age web page that will test you and give you your real age.)

I know a man—who seems the picture of health—but he has never worked out. He's in his 60s, but his real age came out at 85! I also know several married couples in their late 60s and even 70s who have a real age somewhere in the 50s.

But let's get back to some of the high-quality parts of a marriage and finish the discussion about sex and marriage. A good sexual experience requires stamina, especially with age. The sexual experience at 60-plus can be the most satisfying of your life—if you're in shape. Males, who finished a sexual encounter in only a few minutes when they were in their 20s, are able to extend the experience to 30 or 40 minutes, and if the foreplay is added in, to sometimes for an hour. It is truly one of the few benefits of growing older.

Vertis and I have had a wonderful sex life from its inception, and, when we were young, many times intercourse was over in minutes. However, that's just part of being young and full of testosterone. But both of us will tell you, that the past 20 years of our sex life—from 50 to 70 have been the best—by far!

Surviving marriage is not just about being around longer with each other. It's about being around with a great quality of life for as long as possible. Who would want to limit a wonderful marriage by being a couch potato and losing your sex life after 60?

I believe that surviving marriage and reaching a plateau of contentment with your mate, is not something you do for 10, 15, or even 30 years. It's something you commit to do for a lifetime. Wouldn't it be better if you and your spouse built up a wonderful loving, absolutely top-quality marriage—a 95th-percentile one—and it lasted for 50 or 60 years instead of having that same marriage slowly dissolve after 20 or 30 years because one or both didn't stay fit?

How much is it worth to you to be able to extend the superior quality of life provided by a exceptional marriage another 20 years? It's hard to put a value on something that is truly priceless. That's why getting the marriage right by marrying the right person is only part of the problem. Extending the perfect marriage as long as possible is the other part of what should be your goal, and you can't do that unless you're fit.

Now, let's look at how much conditioning will help to ensure a good-quality marriage. Yes, it's moderation again. An exercise program that is insufficient to keep you in good physical condition, or one that overtaxes your body, is not a marriage-builder. So what is the optimum amount of exercise needed to keep you in shape for a long marriage?

Hundreds of books have been written about physical fitness, and, if you're a novice in the gym, you should read at least a couple of the more popular ones. I'll only cover the basics in this discussion. First, if you haven't exercised before, be sure you get checked out by a doctor in order to detect any hidden problems that might make it dangerous to work out. After you get your check-up, join a gym, health club or exercise studio—a place that not only offers exercise machines and running tracks, but also has certified trainers on staff to direct you.

However, I know most of you—especially you guys—won't bother to work out with a trainer, so listen up. I have a few pointers for you. First, to protect and strengthen your heart, vascular system and lungs you need to do aerobic workouts. Dr. Kenneth Cooper, of the Cooper Aerobics Center in Dallas, invented the word "aerobic." Aerobic exercise is any activity that increases your heart rate. By working your heart and lungs, you strengthen them and build an overall healthy heart, lungs and circulatory system. The better your aerobic fitness, the more efficiently your heart, lungs and blood vessels transport oxygen throughout your body. Aerobic exercise includes any physical activity that uses large muscle groups and increases your heart rate. Every gym has several types of machines you can use, or you can walk or run outside to get an aerobic workout.

The second critical part of the aerobic exercise regiment, especially if you are a novice, is to begin slowly and gradually build up to where you can reach and maintain your heartbeat at 80 percent of its maximum rate for 30 minutes. Most treadmills have a chart and sensors that tell you, for your age, what your heartbeat should be to reach this 80 percent. Don't jump on a treadmill and, without any workout experience, try to do 30 minutes at 80 percent of your maximum heart rate. It's dangerous to stress your body that much.

Some people, in order to get their aerobic workout, lengthen their workouts by walking instead of jogging or running, and based on many studies, walking produces the same benefits. Either way, a trainer will give you a chart that shows how much of a workout you need to reach this optimum level. You should do aerobics a minimum of three times a week and preferably five times a week. Working out one or two times a week produces very few benefits. If you reach the aerobic workout level as per the chart for your age, and you do the workout at least three times a week, you're over halfway there.

The second part of your workout has to do with body core and overall strength. This is called muscular fitness. Strength training at least twice a week can help you increase bone strength and muscular fitness. It can also help you maintain muscle mass during a weight-loss program. Without strength training, mobility, especially in your later years of life, will decrease at a much faster rate.

Dr. Lipchitz, of the Arkansas Center for Aging, says one of the greatest problems senior adults have is losing their mobility, and they lose it because of the lack of strength training. This is called core stability. The muscles in your abdomen, lower back and pelvis are known as core muscles. Core exercises help train your muscles to brace and protect the spine, enabling you to use your upper and lower body muscles more effectively.

Strength training gives your body an overall fitness level that can't be reached by doing aerobic workouts alone. If someone tells you they only run for a workout—no matter if they're marathon runners—they're not completely fit, and when the running breaks down muscle tissue, ligaments and sometimes bones, then the lack of strength training will come back to haunt them with a vengeance.

Well, how do you do strength training? Basically, strength training is putting stress against individual parts of your body that will cause your muscles to react and strengthen. You can use free weights to develop a lot of your muscle mass, but it takes specialized machines to focus on every muscle group.

Most gyms have weight machines that will do the job, but in order to not injure yourself and to be able to get the maximum benefit from them, you should get initial instructions from a trainer. In order to get the needed benefits for your various muscle groups you must use a number of machines. A trainer will give you the weight amount and the number of repetitions for each machine.

After you get the sequence down you can get the amount of strength workout you need by adding at least two and preferably three 30-minute periods per week of weight work to your routine, and you're on your way to physical fitness.

However, two other items should be included in your exercise program: stretching exercises and balance training. Stretching improves the range of motion of your joints and promotes better posture. Regular stretching can even help relieve stress.

Balance training is also critical, especially as we age when we're susceptible to falls and fractures. You can be strong, flexible and aerobically fit, yet still have poor balance. Try a tai chi class to help maintain your balance.

One final note about workouts and being fit: I'm sorry, but you can't workout for a couple of months and then call it quits. Being physically fit is a lifetime proposition. Jack LaLanne, the famous fitness coach, died at 95, and up until a few months of his death, was working out regularly. However, you can take a vacation from your workouts, and I've found the best way to do this is to take an actual vacation and not do a lick of training—in a gym. At least that's what Vertis and I do. When we're on vacation, we walk, and I mean walk. In New York City, we never take a cab—10 blocks is nothing. By the time we return to the gym from vacation, we're fresh and ready to start our regular routine again, and after only a few days, we'll have built back up and returned to the fitness level we had before leaving.

Well, being physically fit is only one part of good health. In order to reach your goal of making it into the elite 95th percentile, you need to be more than physically fit—you must be healthy. We'll cover that in the next chapter.

Premise # 6
You must be healthy

Healthy

That's right, I'm not through with writing about being fit to survive marriage. There is a lot more to being fit than just having strength and stamina. A person can be physically fit, but a walking heart attack or stroke waiting to happen. Yes, being physically fit and having the stamina to be a good marriage partner is more than just having muscle strength. It's possible to have strength and yet have underlying problems that will cause debilitating conditions if left alone. High blood pressure, clogged arterial vessels and prostrate problems are just a few of the diseases that have very few early symptoms. I know you've read in the newspapers about cases where a marathon runner drops dead of a heart attack while running. It wasn't the stress of running the marathon that killed him; it was undiagnosed heart disease.

To understand why being healthy is a building block to a quality marriage, let's look deeper into the reasons why the combination of being physically fit inside and out is critical to surviving marriage. This chapter will focus on the part of being fit that we can't see, and addresses the question of why it matters.

Most marriages begin early—in our 20s or 30s, when we are as healthy as we'll ever be. A 20-year-old person's thoughts are focused on many things, but health is usually not one of them. However, keep this in mind: If we're to survive marriage, and obtain a top-quality relationship, we're talking about keeping that relationship for the long term, not the first five years. We all feel invincible in those heady years when we're making love every night, and staying up all hours partying. But those days won't last forever, and if we have a lick of sense, we'll plan for the time when the natural aging process slows us down.

If we don't eliminate the excesses we had in our 20s and 30s, we can be sure they will begin to affect our various organs, and whether we like it or not, Mother Nature and Father Time will slow us down. It's not difficult to look ahead and realize that being unhealthy will cause a number of weaknesses to show up in your body and have a negative impact upon your marriage.

The basic question about a person's health is, "Can you, by being healthy, forestall future marriage problems and extend a high-quality life?" You bet you can. But first, we'll make a couple of assumptions to understand why a marriage, where one or both of the partners are unhealthy, might be in trouble. We'll start by a looking ahead to the day when a couple has been married for 25, 30 or even 40-years.

There are several possible scenarios. First, let's assume that this couple's lifestyle is anything but healthy. They smoke, don't exercise, don't take vitamins or eat properly, and they haven't had a physical examination in years. They've also put on more than a few pounds, and now they weigh 40 pounds more than they did when first married. (I know this sounds grim, but you'd be surprised at how many marriages are exactly in this shape.) How will those marriage hold up under these conditions?

Back to the Atlanta airport—do you think the obese members of the crowd who could be healthy and active have a good-quality married life or a decent sex life? Of course not. It's almost physically impossible. They may still have a marriage, and they may still have sex, but it will be lacking.

Of course, it's not all sex. A lifestyle without proper vitamins, the absence of physical exercise and a lousy diet will increase the risk of prostate cancer and dozens of other problems such as hardening of the arteries, dementia, cancer, emphysema, and osteoporosis. I don't think I have to tell you how much of a negative effect any of those diseases will have on a person's ability to have a top-quality life.

But probably the biggest negative effect which being unhealthy will have on these marriage is very simply this: The partners won't have the ability or the energy to do many of the pleasurable, ordinary things available to them as a couple. As an unhealthy couple ages, they'll find that a number of pleasurable activities they easily accomplished in their 20s and 30s are now simply impossible for them to do.

If you're in a marriage for the long term, as we all intend to be, then it simply makes sense to live the best quality of life for as long as you can. Of course, no one can predict that someone with a super, healthy lifestyle will live longer than someone with an unhealthy lifestyle, but what you can predict this: The healthier the person, the better quality of life that person will have, no matter how long she or he lives.

My mother died at 78 after more than 50 years of smoking finally killed her—I guess that's why I hammer on smoking so much. Her quality of life during the last 10 years dwindled down to where she was in a wheelchair in an assisted living center. If she had lived a healthy lifestyle, she'd have probably lived another 20-years, but, more importantly, the years from 60 to 80 probably would have been quality ones.

I think you'll agree that being healthy is a must goal for every marriage, so how do marriage partners maintain a healthy lifestyle? Again, it's a partnership, and even though a partnership in living a healthy lifestyle sounds a little far-fetched, lets me explain what I mean. First, living healthy in a fast-paced work environment where fast food is at your beck and call is difficult. If husband and wife don't work together, it's very difficult for one to follow the healthy lifestyle while the other tries to pull them in the opposite direction.

In order for a couple to maintain a top-quality marriage and live the best life available to them, they must work as partners to achieve certain health-related goals. The following are certainly not the only things that go into living healthy but they are some of the most important.

Eat healthy

If you've joined a health club and are going five days a week getting fitter every day, it's a good start, but you need to carry it a step further. Consider what would happen to your new diesel Mercedes if you made a mistake and put gasoline in it. Well, it might chug along, but eventually—actually sooner than eventually—it would die a premature death. Yes, cars die, just like we do. It not hard to imagine the average American pulling up to the gas station (fast food place) and filling his or her body with diesel (fat) instead of gasoline (salad).

Yes, they'd continue to chug along, and then, years later, be on the prayer list at church for having an eight-way bypass. So make your marriage partnership a dining partnership and make talking about what you eat on a daily basis an integral part of your conversation with your spouse.

This is not a diet book, but without a healthy diet a marriage partnership can't fulfill its potential. It's a simple premise that an unhealthy diet eventually leads to an incapacitated individual and premature death. It's hard, actually impossible, to have an optimum marriage, if one or both partners aren't fully functional.

There are many diet recommendation, most of which drastically cut down on fat and fried food, and beef up green, leafy vegetables. You can eat healthy, but it's not easy. Over the years, try to slowly cut out fried foods, refined sugar, and red meat.

Those are the big culprits, and the more of those you drop and replace with grains, vegetables, and fish, the healthier you will become.

Get a Physical

I'll be as straightforward as I can: Get a physical on a regular basis, every year if you're over 60—and have your blood work done even more frequently. After getting your physical, ask the doctor to explain the details of your blood work and take a copy home. Don't be satisfied with, "Everything's normal." Understand every item in the blood twenty analysis, and if you have to sit with your physician for an extra 30-minutes, it'll be well worth your time.

But a physical examination is only one part of assuring ourselves that we're fit. Most doctors will include a treadmill test, which is usually sufficient to detect many of the heart problems that come from our American way-of- life. As part of my physical examination, I include a CAT Scan, which is designed to analyze the condition of your body's organs from your lower abdomen to your upper chest. The "CT Scan" will also give you an indication of potential heart and circulatory problems by calculating the calcium buildup in heart-related arteries. I try to get a scan every other year. The new ultrasound examinations are also very helpful in assessing the condition of your interior organs.

Look at getting a physical as part of a preventive medicine program, instead of considering it a tool to diagnosis an already active disease. By paying attention to the results of your blood work, the amount of calcium in your heart arteries, and other findings, you can work to prevent many of the major illnesses that are so prevalent in today's fast-food, chemical-laden world.

Preventive Medicine

The next part of being healthy is to do everything you can to prevent diseases. It's called Preventive Medicine—trying to stop an illness from happening rather than treating it after it attacks your body. This makes perfect sense, but you would be surprised at how many individuals scoff at adding preventive medicine to their healthcare equation.

I'll state it as simply as I can: If you don't have a healthy lifestyle diet, which probably includes vitamins and mineral supplements, then even by being physically fit, you may still fall short of your overall fitness goal. Sometimes the little things we ignore year after year build up and cause terrible health problems.

Many books have been written on ways we can use preventive medicine to avoid diseases that come with bad diets and mineral deficiencies. I'll offer some suggestions later in this chapter. However, if we break down all the necessary ingredients to keep us healthy, they include a broad range of items that work together to give you an overall healthy body.

A healthy lifestyle, which leads to a healthy body, can be broken down into several easily understood do's and don'ts. Of course, we already know many of the don't: don't smoke, don't do drugs, don't drink excessive amounts of alcohol or eat a lot of fatty, high-cholesterol food and cut down on sugar and carbohydrates. That is an abbreviated version of the high-value don'ts. If you do nothing else but eliminate the big don'ts in your lifestyle, you'll have taken a giant step toward optimum health.

That's the easy part of the health equation, and we all understand it. However, it's unfortunate, that even with all the understanding about what causes bad health, most Americans ignore all or part of the big don'ts. Since our goal is not to just be part of the pack but to lead the pack, we must sort out the little do's and don'ts. By micro-managing our bodies, we can ward off many of the ordinary health problems that human beings face. We should start by diligently assessing our bodies needs, and when we do that, we'll see that most individuals could do more to prevent disease and thereby enhance their health

Therefore, our question becomes: How can we use preventive medicine to build up our overall health? And the second part of the question is: Should we take vitamins and mineral supplements as part of our preventive medicine regime and, if so, how much?

To answer those questions we must recognize the differences in our bodies. Our bodies are all unique and some of us need supplements on a regular basis that others don't. Most of the time the need for supplements and vitamins is not obvious, and since every body's genetic makeup is different the needs of each body are different. The idea behind vitamins and mineral supplements is very simple: It is to give our body anti-oxidants and other supplements to help the body fend off disease and compensate for any deficiencies that may be present—and in doing so develop a healthier body that is more resistant to disease.

Of course, my own recommendation is to take vitamins and mineral supplements. Forget all you've read about getting all the vitamins you need from what you eat. Everyone's body is different and what your body needs at a specific time in your life may be a lot different than someone else's. In addition, your body's needs may change many times during your lifetime. A deficiency you develop at 50 might not have been there at 20 or 30.

The overall approach to good health is a combination of many factors. That's why I recommend using a physician who believes in a holistic approach to well-being. Now I know that just the word holistic scares some folks: "Oh, God, he's one of them New Age weirdoes who's going to have us eating seaweed." Yes, maybe, but what if seaweed has some of those trace elements your body is woefully missing and just the taking of a seaweed pill kept you from getting cancer? Well, duh—yes, I'd take seaweed pills for the rest of my life if it kept me from getting cancer. How about you? (But you know, I can't say if seaweed pills will keep you from getting cancer, and neither can anyone else.)

Let's face it, every human body is different and the differences are so subtle that even the most detailed examination can't tell everything about what vitamins or food supplements we need. One thing, though, is certain: With the lifestyle that we are all a part of, it's almost impossible to get every nutrient your body needs by just eating a healthy diet. On top of that we are exposed to thousands of disease-causing chemicals in our processed foods and the air we breathe.

So what do you do? I think you err on the side of excess. Well, at first blush that sounds a little off the wall, but here's the rationale. By not knowing when our bodies are literally screaming for some trace nutrient, we could be inadvertently opening up a weakness that could cause us to contract some illness, or at the least reduce our optimum health.

Of course, you can't just stuff yourself with vitamins on the theory that if some are good for you, then more is better. No, that won't work, because even though our bodies are extremely efficient and much of what we ingest is just passed through, some vitamins are absorbed into the body and can build up and cause harmful reactions. So, to be sure you're not loading up on something—whether its food supplements or vitamins—that can cause you harm, have your physician look at your list of vitamins and food supplements.

However, remember, you're looking for problems with buildup and negative bodily reactions caused by certain vitamins, not a recommendation about whether or not you should be taking vitamins. Most physicians are not well-versed in a holistic approach to medicine and the minuscule number of nutrition courses they take in medical school are not enough to prepare them to make a judgment on whether or not to take vitamins.

Now, let's look a little deeper into preventive medicine. Scientific research has proven that there are many supplements on the market today that add to our body's ability to resist debilitating diseases. Most of the "do" items enhance our health by being preventive, disease-fighting supplements Anything we can do in order to prevent disease is a thousand times more effective than treating a disease after we have symptoms. Whole books have been written on which vitamins and mineral supplements are helpful in preventing certain diseases. By consulting your physician and a nutrition expert, you can develop a list of supplements and vitamins that will fit your body's makeup.

Over the years, Vertis and I have developed a list of vitamins and mineral supplements we believe are helpful in maintaining our health. Some of these have been recommended by physicians, others by dietitians and health- food experts. And on our own, we have researched the benefits of numerous vitamins and mineral supplements to determine their beneficial effects.

However, before you take any supplement, it's wise to research the benefits and side effects and consult your physician about any possible toxic buildups. Some of today's doctors are much more conscious of preventive medicine than physicians a generation ago, and many of them actually prescribe a regimen of vitamins and minerals. Physicians at the highly regarded Cooper Clinic in Dallas have even developed vitamin and mineral supplements that they recommend to their patients. However, some doctors don't, and I would be wary of a physician who tells you, "You don't need to take vitamins and mineral supplements. You get plenty in a balanced diet."

My take on vitamins and mineral supplements goes something like this: Every person is a unique vessel, and what one person requires for maximum health may vary greatly from individual to individual. A number of studies have found that a great number of debilitating illnesses are caused by a lack of certain minerals or vitamins. Of course, good examples are the early sailors who contracted scurvy on long voyages because they were deprived of vitamin C; when limes were added to their daily ration of food, the scurvy disappeared.

Who's to say, or how do you know, if your body is lacking in some vital nutrient? Well, the short answer is that many times we don't know until our bodies break down and we have the disease. And even then many times we can't pinpoint the deficiency. Below is my personal list of vitamins and mineral supplements. I don't have the space to detail out all the potential benefits from these supplements, but just check them out online or in reputable reference books and you'll have more information than I could possible give you.

Richard's Daily Vitamins and Mineral Supplements

(1)At breakfast a handful of walnut halves—(13-8 pieces)—lowers cholesterol prevents heart disease

(2) 1000 mg of natural pomegranate capsules or juice and a half cup of blueberries, a proven antioxidant, to go with my breakfast granola.

(3)CoQ10—100 mg for heart health

(4)Zinc complex, 50 mg plus 2.5 mg copper (guys only) for prostate health

(5) Glucosamine Chondroitin MSM 750 mg (2) for joint support

(6) E 400 IU for heart health and to thin blood

(7) One capsule of multi-vitamin and mineral supplement with iron

(8)Super milk thistle (2) for liver support

(9)DMAE to promotes sound sleep and healthy skin

(10) Folic Acid 800 mg (2) for cholesterol control

(11)Sockeye salmon oil 1000 mg and Omega 3 for protection against peripheral artery disease

(12)One low-dose aspirin to help prevent blockage in heart arteries

(13) Lutein for your eyes, advanced 24 mg

(14)Revatrol—a red wine extract—for heart and longevity

(15)C complex with bio-rose blend, an antioxidant complex—1000 mg

(16)Grape seed antioxidant—100 mg

(17)Chromium—200 mg, helps prevent diabetes

(18)Super Saw Palmetto (2 capsules) 160 mg (men only—prostate health)

(19)B-6—25 mg; B-12—500 mg

(20)Drisdol—vitamin D—regulates calcium and other minerals, promotes bone development

(21)Selenium—200 mg;

(22)Calcium—bones—prevents obstreperous

(23)A concentrated vegetable and fruit capsule—an antioxidant.

Yes, I know you're thinking "that's a big handful," and it is. However, each of the pills I swallow has some documented benefit. I try to spread them out over three meals to allow my digestive tract to better absorb them.

The Polypill

As I was writing this book I received an e-mail from my brother, Dr. William Mason of Little Rock. The e-mail was a forward from Mayoclinic.com. I think the information it contained was significant enough to include in this section on preventive medicine.

Question from a patient: "Polypill: Does it treat heart disease? What is the Polypill? Can it prevent or treat heart disease?"

Answer from Martha Grogan, M. D.

The term "Polypill" describes a pill that's a combination of several medications commonly used to treat heart disease and high blood pressure. Doctors aren't sure what exact combination of medications should be included in a Polypill. It's thought that low doses of each of these medications could be effective:

Aspirin

Water pills (diuretics)

Medications to make your heart beat with less force (beta blockers)

Medications to help keep your blood vessels open (ACE inhibitors)

The Polypill is still being studied, and isn't available for sale yet in the United States. Who should take the Polypill is a controversial issue. Doctors are still trying to see if the Polypill should be given as a preventive measure to people who haven't had a heart attack or stroke, or as a treatment option for people who have already had a heart attack or stroke.

The internet is loaded with articles about the Polypill and some studies indicate, if the new trials in Europe are successful, that the Polypill could reduce heart-related illnesses by as much as 80 percent.

I'm already taking three of the five medications in the Polypill, and if the FDA approves the pill, I'll be one of the first to add it to my preventive medicine regime.

Going Beyond the Ordinary

When it comes to health, I believe that everyone who can should be on the cutting edge of treatments and supplements. If you search the internet, hundreds of treatments pop up for almost every disease known to man. In addition, countless sites promote wellness by unorthodox methods. I think, for some individuals, these treatments may be beneficial. Many swear by certain supplements that haven't received FDA approval, saying the government's process for certifying them for use by the public is too slow. That indeed may be the case, since many drugs that haven't received FDA approval are already in use in Europe. However, I would use extreme caution and research the side effects very carefully, if you are considering any unapproved drugs or supplements. (Numerous supplements, hormones, and other treatments don't require FDA approval, and many of these have strong supporters.)

Some of the more controversial items I have listed below. Naturally, with any hormone, food supplement or other substance that you bring into your body, there are potential positive and negative effect to consider. Many people have decided the benefits derived from using the substances listed below greatly exceed the negatives—or side effects. Let me give you an overview of some of the most popular ones.

DHEA is a popular additive that has both proponents and opponents. Positive effects have to do with the stimulation of natural body hormones, especially the production of testosterone in males. This product is especially helpful in older men because the production of testosterone in the human body gradually decreases as a person ages. Low testosterone levels equate with a low sex drive.

Many men have seen age-related hormone loss render their sex life almost non-existent. The erectile dysfunction drugs are of little use if the testosterone- induced sexual desire is not there. In study groups, the addition of DHEA has helped increase the production of testosterone in males and rejuvenate their sexual activity, but not without some possible side effects. The most troubling of these side effects is the stimulation of the male prostate gland, which may cause enlargement, and, if early stages of cancer are present, the growth of cancer cells. For this reason many doctors will not recommend DHEA as a regular dietary supplement.

Testosterone Replacement

Testosterone replacement is another way to restore an active sex life. Testosterone is partially responsible for the sex drive in both men and women. According to some studies, the loss of testosterone robs men of their energy, strength and libido. And according to several studies, testosterone therapy can restore healthy sexual excitement to youthful levels in both men and women. Following are some of the benefits attributed to testosterone therapy: lowers cholesterol, improves memory, elevates mood, protects against heart disease, enhances sex drive, builds lean muscle, improves sexual performance and increases energy.

What is the best way to get testosterone? One of the new ways is for a doctor to surgically insert several small time-release tablets into the body via a very small incision. This testosterone is slowly released into the blood over a period of several weeks. A physician can check the testosterone level in your blood to determine the number of testosterone pellets needed. Depending upon the individual, three or four pellets must be inserted every six weeks.

After interviewing one lady friend about her husband's diminishing sex drive and its resurgence after testosterone replacement, I can tell you she is completely convinced this therapy works. According to her, it reversed her spouse's low sex drive and restored the couple's intimacy.

However, many of the same side effects associated with DHEA are present in testosterone replacement therapy, so be sure you understand the wide range of possible secondary responses before you begin the therapy.

Human Growth Hormone

HGH is another supplement that many people swear by. This is an attempt to restore the naturally occurring growth hormone in your body, a hormone that reduces with age. By taking the HGH shots, many individuals report a better sense of well-being. In addition, the hormone stimulates muscle growth and restores an active sex life. In fact, testimonials from numerous subjects have compared HGH to a miracle drug. Some of the benefits of HGH are: Controls obesity and reduces your chances of getting Type 2 diabetes. It also has shown to improve cardiac and lung functions which lowers blood pressure.

Many people believe the benefits far outweigh the side effects. But there have been severe side effects present in some individuals who take HGH. The side effects include, joint pain, fluid retention, abnormal bone and cartilage growth, and an irreversible insulin resistance. Insulin and HGH always counteract so they cannot tolerate each other in the same body. A long-term abuse of HGH treatments, especially with athletes, has been documented to lead to some deadly and sometimes fatal conditions. Some of these problems include irregular heart rhythm, enlargement of internal organs such as the liver, kidneys and the heart, as well as joint and facial deformities and a complete shutdown of the pituitary gland.

Naturally, with that many possible side effects an individual must use extreme caution and be under a doctor's supervision while taking HGH. A word of caution: If you decide to take the hormone, do it not only under a doctor's supervision but also for a limited time. The longer you take the hormone, the greater the chances of side effects.

***

A final note on these more controversial hormones: I do not have the expertise to recommend any of these hormones. I advise that they only be taken under a doctor's supervision and for a limited time. Another note of caution: Don't focus on the benefits and ignore the side effects. Be fully aware of what you are putting in your body and then judge if it is something you are comfortable with—weigh the pros and cons. Remember, the goal is to do everything you can to build up your body to remain healthy for as long as possible.

Let me give you an example of why you should do everything you can to maintain a high quality of life. My wife and I were traveling in Hungary many years ago before the Berlin wall fell and Eastern Europe achieved democracy. After dinner one night we retreated to the wine cellar in our hotel for a nightcap. A young man served us, and then after a few pleasantries, sat down and joined us, eager to talk with Americans. We had a delightful conversation and got a real insight into the dark, dreary world of Communism. In our conversation, smoking and exercising were mentioned, and we told him that we didn't smoke, and that we ran or worked out at least four or five days a week. He didn't understand why. As the conversation continued we tried to explain that we felt better and could enjoy life more, if we stayed healthy. Then he uttered one of the saddest lines I've ever heard in my life: "Well, there's no reason to be healthy here. We don't have anything to live for."

Look at your marriage in light of that statement. If you're healthy, and if your marriage has worth and you treasure the moments you spend with your spouse, wouldn't you want as many moments with him or her as possible? Sure you would. That's why being healthy is key to surviving marriage.

So if you're in great health when you reach that ultimate plateau of a pleasurable and joyous marriage, you will have the ability to possibly extend it for extra decades. That should encourage you to work on these key marriage principals. Remember, your goal is to get in that top 95th percentile, and stay there as long as you can.

Premise # 7
You must have a healthy lifestyle

A Healthy Lifestyle

Now, let's talk about another part of overall fitness—the lifestyle equation. It's how and why you should be involved in a healthy lifestyle. We mentioned earlier that moderation in some things—such as having an occasionally martini—wouldn't have a great effect on an overall healthy lifestyle. However, the key here is to not see how many of the negatives your body can stand, but to guide your lifestyle in the direction of truly healthy activities. Many activities that encourage healthy lifestyles, and I don't have to list them for you. Most of them make common sense, and you're certainly aware of them.

So for the rest of this chapter I want to review the lifestyles that are destructive to a quality life. I believe it's the cumulative, negative factors—the destructive parts of an unhealthy lifestyles—that threaten your marriage. In other words, if you add up all the items in your diet each one individually wouldn't substantially affect you health. However, if one dish of ice cream is added to a helping of fried potatoes, which goes along with a martini, and then a cigar after dinner—you have a problem. And that problem is the result of the cumulative effect of the listed items—and believe me, it will adversely affect your marriage and, without saying, your quality of life.

Let me explain what I think is a unhealthy lifestyle. An unhealthy lifestyle is not necessarily one where all fitness activities are ignored. Sometimes just the environment in which you participate in an activity is important. Sitting in a smoky bar or standing with a group of friends who smoke can be a negative to your health—and your marriage. Recent studies show that breathing secondhand smoke for as short a time as 30 minutes can cause your heart arteries to constrict. Yes, and believe it or not, there are still smoky bars and certainly a lot of smoky casinos out there. If you sit there night after night sipping beer, watching football, kibitzing with your buddies, or shoving quarters into a slot machine, it's destructive to your marriage. It's not part of a healthy lifestyle.

I know you thinking that breathing secondhand smoke is all I'm talking about, but it's not. No, not by a long shot. It's the daily, or I might say nightly, separation from your spouse that is also destructive. Of course, breathing all that secondhand smoke is destructive and can lead to a whole raft of physical problems, but the emotional and mental problems are a lot more important than the physical ones here.

If an activity is obsessive—meaning one that takes up an inordinate amount of one spouse's time—that activity will undermine even the most successful marriage. I don't care if you go to the library and read about stamp collecting every night, that's obsessive and destructive to a positive relationship. Sometimes it's hard to even admit you have an obsessive habit or activity, but if a couple will sit down and list every activity, away from work, that they are involved in, and then list the time each activity takes, it will be clear which ones are negative factors in that marriage.

Of course, just acknowledging which lifestyle items are obsessive is not enough. In almost every situation, both partners will have things that are obsessive, or at least taking up a lot of time. If a couple wants to reduce the time involved in these activities, they must compromise. By doing this, the couple will free up quite a bit of time for other common pursuits—things they can do together. This gives the couple an opportunity to add another dimension to their lives by being involved in something positive that will build up the marriage. If a couple does that, then they will have traded a negative for a positive and will have substantially improved their marriage.

The key to a healthy lifestyle is to be involved—preferably with your spouse—in doing things that will enhance you both physically and mentally. So, how do we go about pursuing activities that build up a marriage instead of being involved in things that satisfy only one spouse? First, we must be brutally honest on this one, because if we don't, we won't change. Do not try to rationalize an activity just because you enjoy doing it. Evaluate it in an honest and straightforward manner. Is this activity negative to my health? Is this something that works in a partnership marriage? Is this an activity that is done solely by one of the marriage partners? Is it disliked by the other partner? Does participation in this activity take up an inordinate amount of time? You can go on and on about which activities may have a negative impact on a marriage, but the bottom line is this: If something is a significant negative factor in a marriage, it should be dropped.

But let's be realistic. There will be exceptions in every marriage, and if there is an understanding or some agreement that treats the marriage partners fairly, and if it doesn't create tension in the marriage, the marriage partners can trade off. Still, two negatives don't make a positive. It's not the best solution, but it's sure better than continuing the activity and trying to ignore one partner's feelings.

Well, so much for being fit and involved in healthy lifestyles. I think it's obvious that if you want to reach the highest-quality marriage possible, you must be not only healthy, but also involved in healthy activities. If you aren't, you can't possibly be in the elite 95th percentile.

Premise # 8
Your appearance is a building block for a high-quality marriage

Appearance

In the last several chapters I've written about being healthy, and how important a healthy lifestyle is to your marriage. However, there are other related factors that contribute to a good-quality marriage. Believe it or not, your physical appearance is important—very important. And I don't mean just while you're young and under 30. Part of building a good-quality marriage should be to maintain as much of your mature, attractive appearance—your overall physique and facial features—for as long as practical.

But evidently, from the looks of some couples around the big box stores, quite a few folks consider "practical" to be until something droops or extends or wrinkles. No, that's not what I mean. We all know that with the passage of time, our bodies change. We can't reverse aging, but we can slow it down, and with a little work we can make the best out of what Mother Nature gave us.

Many couples get complacent about their appearance as they pass 50, and I'm sure you can name numerous marriages where one or both marriage partners have essentially thrown in the towel, appearance-wise. Is appearance important in building a good-quality marriage relationship? Yes, I believe it is, and as you read this chapter, I hope I can convince you why. This is my take: Appearance is not an absolute in a marriage, but it is important. Yes, I know Hollywood has given us a distorted view when it comes to a person's appearance, but I still believe that if you want to extend and build a good-quality marriage, you'll do everything you can to look attractive and desirable. Let's consider my marriage for a moment.

Vertis is 68, and she could pass for 45—and does. Yes, she's had a little nip and tuck here and there, and she works out vigorously five days a week, but more than that, she cares about her personal appearance. She didn't chop her hair off when she passed 50 nor did she stop dressing fashionably. Along the way she made a habit of consulting with dermatologists and those in the cosmetics industry to take advantage of their expertise. That's one of the keys to appearance that I will emphasize in this chapter: Don't hesitate to get professional help when you need it, and can afford it.

But back to why your appearance is important to your marriage.

In this chapter I want to take a good look at personal appearance and discuss how it's a positive factor in keeping a marriage viable, and how it improves the quality of a marriage. Since we've already talked about being healthy, we'll assume you're as fit as you can be in midlife. But before we look at the things we can do to maintain our personal appearance, let's discuss why it will improve your marriage.

The first and foremost reason to look good is is to please our life partner, not the men or women down at the office. Consider what you thought about your appearance when you were dating. How important was it for you to maintain your personal appearance when you were wooing your spouse? Remember when just a blemish would give you a shudder of distress?

That may be stretching the point, but the basic premise is what matters. We've all seen people who tie the knot and then for all practical purposes just let themselves go. I believe that's certainly not the way to attain a top-quality marriage.

Think back on the mental attitude you had when you were dating. If you can restore that positive mental attitude concerning your appearance, you'll have a good starting point. Okay, let's say you've decided to have that proper mental attitude, then how can you get a realistic opinion about what you need to do in order to improve or maintain your looks? Get ready—and you may not like this recommendation: Let your spouse tell you what you need to do to improve your appearance.

You spouse can see things in your appearance that your friends either ignore or have become complacent about. Of course, this will only work if the partners are brutally honest with each other. Having an honest appraisal is a great starting point to improving your appearance. Ask your spouse to tell you the truth, or it won't work.

But back to the question: Why should you keep up your personal appearance for your spouse, or for that matter for anyone? Consider this fact: Whether it's a male or female, an attractive mate is a plus in any marriage. It's as basic as looking desirable, but it's more than looking great in a sexual manner. Of course, if a husband or wife is appealing and still looks sexy in their later years, it will act as a continuing enhancement to sexual activity. But it's a lot more than that. I think the best way to describe it is to say that taking care of your looks can be a physiological boost to the marriage.

Marriage is so much more mental than we can imagine. Many times we think marriage fulfillment boils down to a list of things we do, or how we react to each other. That's just the tip of the marriage iceberg. The mental satisfaction that is present in a high-quality marriage is paramount. It's the grease that moves the marriage along and smoothes out the bumps. Without this mental and emotional bond, you only have a shell of a marriage and a legal document.

But back to why you should look good. Sometimes it's this simple: It gives me a sense of pride and satisfaction to walk into a restaurant and see that Vertis is being noticed by other men. I guess it's like, "Hey, how about this catch?" It leads to a confidence that spills over into almost every part of the marriage relationship. Sex is better, conversation is livelier, and the marriage takes on an overall attitude of success. And believe me, a positive mental attitude in a marriage is a big part of success.

Well, let's talk about specifics—guys first. Okay, gentlemen, we're going to touch on a tricky subject for most men: trying to maintain a more youthful appearance.

I'm going to assume your body is in decent shape. If it isn't, back up a couple of chapters and re-read. What I want to talk about is primarily from the neck up. Well, we know women have been using everything possible to keep their faces youthful since the beginning of time. But men? Guys, before you jump to conclusions, I'm not talking about a total body sculpture or an ultimate facelift, which is an option, but not for most men.

Now, for a bit, this will be guy talk. Fellows, I hate to admit it, but as I walk down the street I see a lot more women who care about their appearance than men. The slim 180-pound guy who was Mr. Everything in high school is now a 240-pounder with a beer belly hanging over his belt. Does he care how he looks? Probably not, or—barring significant health problems—he'd mostly likely do something about it. Does his wife care? You bet she does, but she's probably given up the fight years ago. (Yes, I know there are women who look just as bad, but there seem to be fewer.)

I guess the first thing we all need to get over is our macho complex. That's right, a lot of us have a built-in John Wayne attitude. It's a "Real men don't do facelifts or hair dyes, use face cream, or, heaven forbid, have filler put in the wrinkles on their face." The result: By the time guys reach 60, they look as if they'd married a woman 20 years or sometimes 30 years younger, when in fact they're the same age.

What's the bottom line? Had you rather look like a craggy old man who has baked his face in the sun, when with a little cash and some resolve you can keep up with the women? Guys, if you answer that question "I don't care," then you'll have real problems in following much of the other advice in this book. But if you're open to improving your marriage, and if you want an honest opinion from someone who cares about you and everything you do, ask your wife—and then take her advice.

Okay, so if you're going to take your wife's word, you find out that you need some help. So where do you start? Some improvements are very simple. A short, very tight haircut or completely shaved head is in vogue right now, so you can cut off that thinning mane of gray hair and lop 10 years off your age with the click of a razor. Shaggy, gray hair is an age-marker. Simply put: It makes you look old.

An illustration: About 10 years ago I was partly bald on top with a thick ring of gray hair around the sides. On top of that, I had a full, gray beard. That gray beard and hair aged me. I finally realized it, and, after I cut it off, my 8-year-old grandson and I were looking at some family pictures taken the year before. There was a full-face shot of me with that gray beard and hair. My grandson pointed and said, "That's Jocko when he looked old."

Well, from the mouth of babes! By the way, Jocko, is what my grandchildren call me. I didn't want a Pap Paw, Pa Pa, Grandfather, or some other aging name hung on me. They love calling me Jocko, and I sure think it sounds a lot younger than Pap Paw, etc.

As we think about our appearance, let's think of the easy things we can do to hold a mature, but youthful look. Of course, eliminating gray hair is the most obvious, but little things such as the shoes and clothes we wear (especially the workout clothes) can age you as quickly as gray hair. Look around you and mimic the well- dressed of the next generation down from you. Don't get carried away and drop more than a generation. There is nothing worse looking than someone who is 50 trying to dress like Miley Cyrus, especially if they're a guy!

Do some of the little things first, like getting rid of the gray and dressing younger. You'll thank me later. One other word about hair: If you decide to color your hair, let a professional do it. Cheap, jet-black dye jobs actually age you. You might even want to have the colorist blend color in with your gray hair gradually, over several appointments, until you find a mix that is age-appropriate and attractive.

But now let's go into the other factors that age men. Of course, if you've got a beer belly hanging over your belt, that's a sure way to look old as well as unhealthy. Get rid of it, even if you have to starve yourself, and if that doesn't work, consider liposuction. It'll hurt like hell, but it will take off pounds of fat immediately. (Make sure you consider the risks of any surgical procedure.)

Now, guys, let's assume you have at least a decent-looking body, you've cut off that gray hair and put a little color into the hair that's left. Now we can take a look at what really ages a man—his face. Well, I know you're going to slam this book shut if I tell you to have a facelift, so I'm not, but there's a lot you can do for your face before you have to go under the knife. You should start by sneaking into your wife's night and day cream and smearing a thick layer on your face twice a day—morning and night. Most of the face creams have a sun block so you get not only a skin treatment, but also protection from the sun. Guys, the sun is really tough on your skin, and if you don't protect your face, it'll end up like a leather punching bag and all the other stuff you do won't salvage it.

After you start using face cream, then it time to check out those scowl wrinkles on your brow, beside your nose, and round your eyes. No, it's not time for the knife, but it might be time for Restylane, which is one of several fillers that diminish wrinkles. Well, if you're like me, when I first heard about the wrinkle fillers a few years ago, I backed away as quickly as I could. However, later, as I started really looking at my face, I could see that a reduction in several major wrinkles would certainly help my looks. I had two parallel, grooves on both sides of my nose about 3 or 4 inches long, the normal process of aging of course. I finally got up the courage to let a dermatologist do a little work on those wrinkles.

Fillers are added by injecting an inert substance beneath the wrinkle. The filler increases the volume, which pushes up the skin and appears to eliminate the wrinkle. I waited until we were on a long vacation where, if I came out looking weird, I'd have time to get back to normal. Well, I cautioned the doctor repeatedly, and she did very little in terms of injecting Restylane under those wrinkles. I had before and after pictures that I examined. Yes, there was a noticeable difference, but only if you looked closely at the before picture.

My friends thought I looked rested from the vacation, and after hearing that, I couldn't wait to have another injection, and so I did it about six months later. Since that time I've had several additional injections to not only to reduce the major wrinkles on both sides of my nose (which, by the way are gone) but to other areas of my face that needed filler.

From my point of view, there is a bottom line to looking youthful, and it is directly related to replacing the collagen in your face. To understand the process better, consider the idea behind dermal fillers. It's as simple as answering the question: What is a baby-faced person? That's easy. It's a person who has a round—and yes, you guessed it—a full face!

Well, that begs the question: What makes a round, full baby face change into a wrinkled, aged face? Of course there are a lot of reasons, but the primary one is that during the aging process we lose collagen. Our skin is similar to a balloon stretched over our muscles and bones. If you visualize a balloon full of air and then slowly let the air out, you can understand what I mean. Our skin loses support from the loss of volume and increase in folds—and we call those folds, "wrinkles."

Facelifts essentially pull the excess skin and reduce the wrinkles by reducing the amount of skin. I'm not too keen on this process, because it reportedly hurts like hell—and you look like a zombie for about six weeks as your face heals. I haven't had a facelift, and I'm not planning on having one. There are other ways to fight Father Time.

In my opinion, restoring volume is a much better and less painful way to reduce wrinkles. And actually it makes more sense to me. A good dermatologist will examine your face and then dot and mark areas where they see the need for filler. After being skittish the first time I had it done, I'm now open to as much cosmetic work as my doctor wants to do. When I started at age 65, I had two very deep wrinkles on either side of my nose, wrinkles that extended from about the midpoint of my nose to the side of my mouth. These wrinkles are one of the age-marker wrinkles and whether or not we realize it or not, they flash our age to everyone as they observe our faces.

I've been to four dermatologists over the past five years and all four have worked on those wrinkles, as well as other areas of my face. Today these wrinkles appear to be almost gone and although I sure don't have that baby face I had when I was 20, I look a good 10 to 15 years younger.

In an article in Face Magazine the writer reviews a new facelift called a Y Lift created by Dr. Yan Trokel, a trained maxillofacial surgeon who teaches cosmetic surgery at Mount Sinai Medical School. Dr. Trokel uses a method he calls "structural volumizing." He explains: "Everything—muscle, bone, fat—starts to deflate. Aging is a process of losing volume, not gravity. What we associate with youth in fullness not tautness."

The Y Lift basically increases the volume of your overall face. It is a revolutionary procedure that takes just over an hour with no bruises, cuts or healing. You can go back to work the next day. However, it's not cheap. Below is a quote from Lycra Magazine:

The Y-Lift corrects the sagging mid-section of a face (men and women) and re-apportions facial features-to look like one's youthful self—and not a freak show facsimile.

With strategically placed deeply injected Juvaderm™, (a hyaluronic filler that's FDA approved), a "moldable cheek form" in the malar region is achieved with the added plus of firming up the jaw line and diminishing the folds that can form from the nose to the mouth.

Other big pluses are that there is minimal, if any bruising, no downtime –a key in our busy lives, no anesthesia, and the "lift" which is customized to fit each patient- gradual falls in two years as the filler is absorbed.

As Dr. Trokel noted "…older patients have the most dramatic results…(but) everyone from thirty somethings on up- can do small things to ward off the major procedures."

COSTS: Comparable to our gal pal's seemingless endless Sculptra injections ($5000-$7000. (end of quote from Lycra Magazine.)

Dr. Trokel has been written up in numerous papers and magazines, and testimonials abound as to the success of this treatment.

In 2011, Vertis and I had the Y-Lift, and we were pleased with the results. However, get ready for your billfold to take a big hit. The standard Y-Lift will set you back around $8,400, for what is call an instant facelift—one without any down time.

Dr. Trokel has pioneered a radically new procedure that attacks the loss of volume from deep within the face. Instead of injecting a small amount of filler directly underneath the wrinkles, he makes two holes on either side of your face and then—after injecting some painkiller—he inserts a long tube under the muscle tissue, all the way to the bone. Then he injects filler to increase the overall volume of your face. In the final analysis, this treatment injects almost 10 times as much filler as the traditional shallow filler injections. The result is an overall fullness of the face.

However, there is some pain involved. I went from a two to an eight on a one to 10 pain scale, but for only a few seconds. After the procedure, which took about 90 minutes, we left Dr. Trokel's office and went directly to a restaurant for lunch. Our faces were tender for a few days, but after a week or we were almost back to normal. I'm sold on Dr. Trokel's procedure.

So that's my primary recommendation, for both men and women: Get some volume back in your face, and you'll be shocked at the positive change. However, even the best fillers only last six months, so be prepared to go back for a touch-up a couple of times a year. I've found out from experience that these procedures take a lot less filler and cost less. (Actually, Dr. Trokel's

Y-Life could be a bargain considering the need to have additional filler touch-ups every six-months.)

Fillers, however, are only one of the new products on the market. Botox is probably the best known of these products. Yes, I'm convinced that that this is helpful for many of us. Botox doesn't act as a filler, but it does work on minor wrinkles by numbing the muscles that cause the brow wrinkles and lines around your eyes. The only problem with Botox (for people who can safely use it) is that it only lasts around four months. Then the muscle recovers and the wrinkles come back. However, repeated injections last longer as the muscle becomes slower and slower to recover. Botox is a good tool, but it my opinion, fillers, like Restylane, are a better long-term answer.

Another sign of aging is the area right below your eyes. How many "hollow-eyed" old men have you seen? Plenty I'm sure. Well, that's because the aging process has drained collagen from around their eyes and the result is—naturally—a sunken look. Yes, these hollow-eyed men need filler under their eyes, but not the type that's used for regular facial wrinkles. A special, near-liquid type of filler is used to add a youthful look to those eyes. (Be sure your cosmetic surgeon or dermatologist knows exactly what he or she is doing, though, before you have anything done around your eyes.)

Of course there are drawbacks to using these fillers—yes, for one thing, they're expensive. Depending on your face, a full treatment of both Botox and Restylane will run between $1,500 and $2,000. However, the good news is the price is coming down, and soon I expect $500 will get you a good treatment.

Another drawback to the current group of fillers is that they only last around six months, but that's changing, too. Already in trials are new fillers that promise to extend their life to almost a year, and I am sure in the years to come these products will continue to improve. Some new fillers even cause the body to react and create more collagen which is an extra benefit.

If fillers aren't enough, consider a few more options: A full facelift, contour threads to pull up those sagging jowls, rhinoplasty (nose work), brow lifts, breast augmentation, breast lift, liposuction, tummy tucks, laser treatments (lasers react to color and can remove those brown spots), skin tightening, Botox, and dermal fillers.

Well, that's just a bit of what's available, and let me be blunt: Don't go whole hog on this. Full facelifts are usually so painful and change your appearance so much that many men will regret having it done.

There are at least another dozen ways to slow the visible aging process without a lot of pain and money. Seek out a good cosmetic surgeon, listen, compare, and then choose which of the many options are for you. Remember, guys, you aren't trying to make your face smooth as a baby's butt, but you are trying to keep from looking like you married a woman 30 years younger. Yes, looks matter.

Since we're talking about men right now, let me give you an example of how a lot of men ignore the aging process. Last June I went out for a Father's Day dinner with Vertis and our grown kids. We had a great time, good food and lively conversation. The restaurant was well-designed with several levels of seating; booths, open tables, and a gorgeous bar all laid out in an open, yet separate grouping arrangement.

We were sitting in a booth that was slightly lower than a large corner booth,which I was facing. Two couples were sitting there, and I noticed them immediately. Two beautiful, youthful-looking blondes were having dinner with two old men—or so it seemed. However, that wasn't the case at all. Vertis knew both couples and smiled when I whispered that observation to her. She whispered back, "The woman on the left is older by a couple of years than anyone at the table. Both men are a couple of years younger than their wives."

"Huh?"

Yes, it was another moment of enlightenment. I looked first at the women—naturally. They were well-groomed, dressed in a youthful manner but not overly so. Their faces were mature, but still striking beautiful. They weren't wrinkle-free, but the normal deep wrinkles that come with aging and loss of collagen, and the hollow eyes, were gone. Their hair, while not long, was almost shoulder length, and they weren't wearing glasses. When they left the restaurant, I noticed that both women had good posture, and their legs—especially their calves— were taut and muscular. You could tell they worked out. These two women presented themselves as attractive, poised, and confident.

However, the men were a different story. Both men were farmer-tanned from being outdoors, probably from playing golf. They weren't overweight, but their shoulders slumped. They were obviously flabby and out of shape with small pot bellies and thin arms. They really didn't look that bad from the rear, but when they turned toward us their faces showed their age—and then some.

Both worn gold-rimmed—what I call "old men's" glasses—had very thin, gray hair that was full on the sides and gone on the top with a few scraggly strands hanging down the back of their necks. That was bad enough, but the wrinkles on their faces sealed their age. Deep sagging jowls, crow's feet around hollow eyes, and convex , sunken cheeks. They had deep, side-nose wrinkles extending from just under their eyes all the way down to their lips, and their facial skin had a dull brown leathery look. Yes, they looked every year of their age, which was around 65.

Could they have had a more youthful appearance with a little work? Of course they could have. Would it have made any difference in the way the other patrons of the restaurant viewed them, or more importantly, how their spouses viewed them? Well, part of that question was answered when the two couples left the restaurant.

As the two couples filed out through the crowded restaurant, man after man glanced up and then watched the two women walk out. They were dressed in an attractive manner—even to younger men. However, I would venture a guess the men were essentially ignored by women in the restaurant.

Would your wife or husband appreciate you more if you cared about your appearance? Will being an attractive spouse help your marriage survive? No, not by itself, but it will add a spark to every married couple's sex life, and in doing so will add one more mental building block to becoming your spouse's best friend.

Some couples who can afford the help don't seem to think it's worth the effort, but lately I've seen more and more evidence of a concentrated effort by middle-aged and older couples who are doing a good job of looking younger. A Little Rock dermatologist recently told me that her business has soared over the past several years, and a big percentage of her new customers were men. Hey, guys, maybe we're wising up.

I don't know whether it's just me or not, but I've noticed that there are more outwardly affectionate responses between attractive couples than between couples who don't care about their appearance. Could it be that if some partners don't care about their appearance, then they don't care about other, more important emotional issues that build up a marriage? It seems to me that appearance and emotional well-being in a marriage are intricately linked. Maybe you can have one without the other, but I don't think so.

There's a bottom line to everything, and I think caring about your appearance boils down to one short sentence. Looking as good as you can means you care about your spouse and your marriage. It is one of the many items that link together to build up a top-quality marriage.

Today, my face isn't wrinkle-free, but it has fewer wrinkles and exhibits a more youthful look, thanks to some good work by dermatologists. No, I don't look 25, but some dermatological work has taken a number of years off my demeanor.

Now a word to women: First off, most of you already religiously use face creams, and you've learned long ago not to lie out in the sun, damaging your skin and exposing yourself to skin cancer. Of course, that's a critical step one. However, it seems that many women quit right there. You don't have to look very far to see women who don't work to keep a good-quality personal appearance. A good percentage seem to think appearances don't matter. Some even stop using lipstick, wear their hair in sloppy or matronly ways, just so and ignore many of the age lines that start appearing after 50. Why?

There are many reasons—some of them health-related issues, others financial— but often these appearance problems are a result of laziness. Yes, it is easier to just go to the beauty parlor once a week and get a short, tightly curled and sprayed hair-do, or forget about putting on makeup. But is this your best appearance?

Over the years I've noticed when these women divorce they usually go through a change that's as dramatic as a caterpillar turning into a butterfly. I call it "Back on the Market." Well, for some reason, that comment really ticks off Vertis. But how else would you explain a newly divorced woman who begins to dress stylishly, has a little cosmetic work done, and generally looks better?

I know you ladies might say she feels better after shucking that louse of a husband. Either way, it's an attitude change and that's what a good-quality marriage must have when it comes to appearance. The husband or wife who doesn't care about their looks, gives the attitude that they don't care about their marriage.

So, really, where does surviving marriage and building a quality life by looking good come in? It's simple, and for two related reasons. Of course, the first is to be an attractive lover for your husband or wife to desire. That's important and even though he or she may tell you looks don't matter, they do. The spouse that wakes up shocked when their mate leaves with an attractive other person realizes the importance, but it's too late.

I know we shouldn't put so much emphasis on a person's physical appearance, but for as long as history has been recorded, both men and women have been preening to attract each other. Even birds have been doing it since creation; they make themselves more attractive to encourage sexual activity. It's not going to change, so get on board and do the best you can with your physical appearance, and when you need a little help, there are numerous ways out there to enhance your looks.

Of course, being more sexually desirable is only one of the reasons to care about your appearance In a long-term marriage it's important to do what you can to enhance and maintain sexual desire by being attractive to your spouse. After all, a vigorous sex life is a primary building block to a top-quality marriage and if that is so, you want to maintain its vigor for as long as possible. That sounds a little basic, but let's be honest: Almost everything having to do with sex is basic. We aren't doing it much differently than our ancestors.

But there are at least two other reasons to keep your looks, and this these may surprise you. First, we mentioned looking good for your spouse, which is certainly important, but looking good for your personal self-image is even more so. You are the greatest beneficiary from maintaining your appearance. If you look good, then you have confidence, and confidence equals improved attitude. And believe me—attitude matters.

But that's not all you gain. When people feel good about themselves, it spills over into every aspect of their lives. Yes, you will want to stay physically fit and looking good because you will feel good about yourself, your attitude toward your family will improve, and your desire to have a high-quality marriage will follow right along.

Looking good is important for those reasons and for many more, which I didn't touch on. After all, the whole idea of this book is for us to live that best life possible, and my premise is that being happily married to the right man or woman is the best way to do that. And looking your best in part of the package. It's just one more step in making it to the elite 95th percentile.

Before we go to the next chapter, I want to clear the air a bit. Some of the advice I've given so far, and other suggestions I'll give in later chapters, won't fit every marriage. Just as every man and woman on Earth has a unique set of fingerprints, every marriage is different. It's up to you to decide how to apply the recommendations I've outlined that has made our marriage a remarkable relationship.

Thank goodness we're all different. What if we all reacted the same way to stimuli? That would make for dull, predictable marriages that would die from the lack of spontaneity. What I'm really trying to say is that some of the precepts that have worked in my marriage may not work in yours. And this chapter on appearance is a good example. Is a person's appearance the key to desirability? In other words are we attracted to people strictly on the basis of their looks?

Yes, I know we all marry for intelligence and wit—yeah, sure. Actually, polls have shown less than 30 percent of American men would agree they wanted a vamp model whose foremost abilities were on view for all to see. In this same survey, marrying for intelligence came out much higher, at over 50 percent. So use this book like your a cafeteria tray, and pick out the items that fit your personality. However, just keep this in mind: the more successful marriage features you can adapt to your marriage, the better your marriage will be.

In the last several chapters we've talked about how healthy lifestyles and proper fitness improve the quality of our marriage. I've also discussed how diet and exercise and good grooming skills can make the best of what we were endowed with, and I've touched on what I call helping Mother Nature.

Will an attractive appearance help your marriage? Yes, but only incrementally. Too much emphasis on appearance can backfire because it encourages obsessive behavior. Just remember not to minimize appearance. It is one of several building blocks which builds a top marriage—and a good-quality life.

Premise # 9
Giving—as in gifts—will strengthen your marriage

Give Gifts

We're a gift-giving nation. Many stores make most of their annual profits around the gift-giving season between Thanksgiving and Christmas, and the card, florist, and other companies have managed to put dozens of reasons for giving gifts on our calendars. Then, when we add traditional birthdays, anniversaries, graduations and Bar Mitzvahs, it seems as if we're overloaded with opportunities for presents. (Yes, I agree with those who say the gift-giving business has been so commercialized that most of the special days mean very little. It almost makes you want to skip all of them.)

However, if you want to keep peace in the family, you'd better not take that attitude. Actually, there's nothing wrong with giving gifts for any of those occasions, but those aren't the type of gifts I'm writing about. Before we look at what I am talking about, let's look at the average marriage when it comes gift-giving.

The normal gift-giving in a marriage usually consists of giving the obligatory gifts. Don't forget that birthday or, anniversary. That's right. Don't forget any special, personal occasions. Your spouse may tell you it doesn't make any difference to her or him, but it does. Well, you might shake your head and say, "Oh, you don't know my spouse." But I do know your spouse, because every spouse has some basic needs and emotions that are somewhat fulfilled by receiving a gift.

Your marriage partner might not do a flip when you present him or her with a special, thought-out gift. And trying to detect any one of the hundreds of suppressed emotions that a human body is capable of may be impossible. However, you can be sure that if you buy your spouse something that he or she knows you took some extra thought in selecting, the reaction, while maybe not noticeable, will be positive. Not only will it be positive, it will be cumulative!

In other words, each special gift will build upon the other as a positive, emotional enhancement to your marriage Believe me, gift-giving, when done properly, can build up even the shakiest marriage.

Now, let's define the proper way to give gifts. We've all seen the sugar-daddies in the movies lavish some cute chick with jewels and fur coats.—for what? Well, I don't think I need to answer that. The gift-giving I'm writing about is 180 degrees removed.

Well, a gift is a gift you might say, but you'd be wrong. In a marriage, relationship gifts take on different emotional meanings from other gifts that may be given to friends or children. Since gifts within a marriage take on emotional ties, they must be the right gift for the occasion. To understand why one gift might be wrong and another one right on target, we must understand some of the emotional strings that are attached to gifts within a marriage.

Obviously, underlying the whole concept of marriage gift-giving is that it will enhance the emotional ties from the recipient to the presenter. The wrong gift might be something the marriage partner takes for granted. And if the gift is taken for granted, there will be little emotional response from the partner receiving the gift.

To understand how marriage gifts influence marriage emotions, consider that there are certain aspects of our marriage we all take for granted. It may be just the inner thought that your marriage partner loves you. If that's the case then, a gift that is expected and taken for granted—such as a box of candy for Valentine's Day—will have a zero emotional response.

Okay, now let's look at an emotionally positive gift-giving experience. If you're expecting a list of good gifts, you won't find them in this book. That's because a positive gift-giving experience within an individual marriage varies from one marriage to the next. Human emotions are so complex that a perfect gift in one marriage would be a terrible selection in another. It's almost impossible to qualify a positive gift without understanding the complex emotional ties within a particular marriage. If that's the case, then each marriage partner must be the one to decide what is the perfect gift for the occasion. Now let's see if we can understand how to give gifts that will build up the positive ties within a marriage.

Gift-giving is just another tool in the marriage relationship, and like other things that enrich a marriage, gift-giving should enhance as many of the positive aspects of the relationship as possible. If that premise is kept in the forefront, and each partner consciously tries to build up these positive emotions, then you will give the right gift and your marriage will blossom.

Gift-giving can have such a positive effect on a marriage that it's hard to keep from over-emphasizing it. Receiving the right gift from a marriage partner is different than receiving a gift from just an acquaintance. Gift-giving in a marriage relationship carries with it an emotional response from both the giver and the receiver—or at least it should.

In order to trigger that emotional response, we must consider the care and thought process that went into acquiring a particular gift. Something that took extra time and reflects some special want your spouse has is 10-times better than an expensive gift you picked out from a catalogue. Don't ever think your spouse won't know where your gift came from and how much it costs. About 30 seconds on the internet will enlighten any questioning spouse.

But back to receiving a positive emotional response: In order to give a gift that will trigger such a response, that gift must be truly personal and well thought-out. The underlying emotional pull is obvious. Very simply put: It will show your spouse that you care. It reflects a desire to please, not an obligation to come forth with a gift on a certain day. It boils down to caring about the desires of your spouse in contrast to giving an obligatory present that is given because you'll be in trouble if you don't.

Positive gift-giving should always trend to the personal—no toasters or vacuum cleaners, no matter how much your spouse needs them. If the gift isn't personal, it will trigger about as much emotional response as paying the water bill.

We've all fouled up in gift-giving. Sometimes the gift is just totally wrong for the occasion, like giving a guy a tie for his anniversary gift. (Actually giving a guy a tie in today's world is always inappropriate.) A bad gift signals several things: (1) You're cheap. (2) You don't care about the occasion. (3) You're too busy to care about the recipient. and when you give a gift that elicits a negative response you are damaging your marriage, not building it up. No gift is better than a bad gift.

Here's a tip when thinking about the right type of gift. The number-one item you should consider is the emotional part of the occasion. Take Valentine's Day or your Anniversary: The items that immediately come to mind are candy and flowers. Both are dead wrong unless you want a paying-the-water-bill response. They are so expected that all you will get is a yawn and an "Oh, yes, thanks—ready for dinner?" That gift is not necessarily a bad gift, it's closer to a no gift. You gave the obligatory gift and your spouse nodded. Someone wasted a few bucks because the recipient had almost no emotional response to receiving the gift—and if the giver of the gift had thought about it, he or she would understand why.

This is a cut-and-dried rule: You should never give candy for Valentine's or roses for an anniversary. Why? Because they're expected! This leads us to the key in gift-giving. It's so simple you can say it in one short sentence: Make your spouse expect—and anticipate—the unexpected. Flowers and candy are the expected gifts, and they can actually be worse than no gift. Guys, if your wife is working her buns off on a diet, and you drop a five-pound box of chocolates on her, she may throw them at you. Bad gift! Go back three spaces on your route to a good-quality marriage. And, ladies, if you run out at the last minute and buy that tie, don't expect to hugged and kissed, especially if your husband quit wearing ties five years ago.

On occasions such as these, your marriage partner will automatically appreciate an unexpected gift because they know it took extra time and consideration. Every time you do the unexpected you will move a notch up toward a top-quality marriage. But not all unexpected gifts are the right gifts. A mess of catfish to clean is sure unexpected, but don't go there, guys, and that goes for anything to do with house or yard work. In this chapter the "Oh my gosh!" unexpected gifts are the ones I want to emphasize—the gifts with the knockout emotional punch. Those are the real gifts. All the others are just ho-hum.

Let's look at real gift-giving, and I think you will understand how giving with emotions involved can strengthen your marriage. Remember this premise—the gift should have emotions attached and should be unexpected. Forget the cost—(but nothing cheap!) and concentrate on the emotions of gift-giving.

A few real-life examples might be helpful here. We built our dream home on the edge of town on property that once was an old farm. By the time we purchased the property the farmhouse was in disrepair and falling down. We cleared it and built a new house on the site. However, not all of the old farm vanished with the dilapidated farmhouse. Every spring, the daffodils that were planted more than 70 years ago pop up and bloom along the abandoned fencerow on the edge of the property.

When I see the daffodils blooming, I know spring is just around the corner and winter will soon be a memory. However, just the sight of a long row of yellow daffodils blooming gives me the opportunity to give an unexpected gift. Some afternoon, while Vertis is at the grocery store or away from the house for a few hours, I'll pick as many as I can and treat her to a big vase of bright, yellow daffodils when she returns home.

Now, I'm not going to tell you that a hand-picked bouquet of flowers by itself will strengthen your marriage, but it is a start. And if built upon, a gesture like this one will show very positive results. The flowers costs me nothing, but a few minutes of my time. Vertis appreciated them, not only for their beauty, but because she knew that with every daffodil I picked I was thinking of her—that's the emotional part of the gift.

That's one of the keys to gift-giving. I call it emotional giving because the gift can be very small and cost very little, but it can elicit a positive emotional response. Do a lot of little gift-giving that is not date-driven and where money is a minor part of the gift. These gifts should be unexpected, and this is an important point: There should be no reason for the gift—and the gift requires thoughtfulness on the part of the giver. To be the type of giving that will enhance the emotional bonds of the couple, these small, thoughtful gifts must be frequent. Then you will benefit from the cumulative emotional buildup that grows with each gift.

Another point to consider when thinking about unexpected gifts: Gifts don't have to be expensive. A text message, card, and even a call from work "just to hear your voice" is a gift. We are conditioned to give a gift that's as expensive as we can afford at Christmas or for special anniversaries. However, you might be surprised at the reception that a little "I was thinking about you" trinket will receive, especially if the note says, "A year ago we spent a weekend in New Orleans. It was wonderful." I guarantee you that gift will be appreciated much more than the same old anniversary flowers, etc. (Of course, if you think about it, the very act of adding frequent, positive emotional responses is the basis for a healthy marriage.) Along the way, I've found that frequent gifts are better than one whopping Christmas or anniversary present. Let me explain: More doesn't mean piling up expensive presents like some sugar daddy. Not at all. If you can regularly surprise your partner with an unexpected small gift—especially when there's not a special occasion coming up—that cumulative gift giving will build and strengthen your marriages emotional well-being. Look at it this way: Every small unexpected gift tells your spouse you took the time to think about them. Remember this: Doing special things are cumulative. In other words one little unexpected gift won't do much, but add to that cards, e-mails, hand-picked flowers, and surprises—all of which show thoughtfulness—and you've moved your marriage up a notch.

If you haven't made it a habit, the first time or two might draw a suspicious look. You've seen the "Why" look before and it's usually because you forgot some special day such as your spouse's birthday. However, after a few of these gifts, your spouse will understand you're giving him or her a gift simply because you thought about them and loved them enough to buy him or her something.

Unexpected gifts are great, but you shouldn't ignore something like a birthday. You should try to make it memorable and thoughtful. Remember this: It doesn't have to cost a lot of money to be the right gift. However, there may be a time when a relative expensive gift is in order.

Let me give you another example of how just another birthday became something that Vertis—and her friends—talked about for weeks. It was very simple. I first told Vertis, on Monday, that it was her birthday week. That's all I said. She smiled, but didn't have a clue what I had in mind.

Her birthday was at the end of the week—Saturday. Later, on Monday afternoon, she received the first of what would be a daily bouquet of flowers—a bouquet every day of her birthday week. The first bouquet caught her off-guard, and she was very surprised and quiet honestly extremely tickled that I would send her flowers nearly a week before her birthday. However, by Wednesday she was ecstatic as the flowers kept rolling in. The very idea that her husband was sending her flowers every day of the week had her friends shaking their heads in disbelief—and envy—while she described the day's bouquet and anticipated the next day's flowers.

On Saturday, her birthday, I sent her seven white roses—her wedding bouquet. Vertis still talks about her birthday week—and so do her friends. The cost? Less than $200 dollars, but the results were worth 10 times that amount. Yes, it did strengthen the affection we have for each other and moved our marriage just a little higher up the emotional ladder.

Let me expand a little more on what I call the element of "something out of the ordinary"—something totally unexpected—out of the blue—no special occasion. That's where you can shine, because of the very nature of the gift. It's the underlying idea that one of the marriage partners was thoughtful and wanted to please his or her spouse, even when there was no special occasion.

I think gift-giving will boost any marriage, if done properly, and the unexpected is the key to building up your positive emotional relationship. We all get into ruts and in a long-term marriage either spouse can guess the gifts given for certain occasions. The "keep 'em guessing" idea of giving when least expected can do wonders to spice up a marriage.

Here's one you might try: Give your partner a tease gift. A gift that recognizes a date a few weeks in the future and reflects back to an anniversary where something special happened to you and your spouse. I'll guarantee you that your spouse will have you on their mind while waiting for the date to roll around. To get the best reaction from this gift, make it romantic, something that refers to the 20th anniversary of your first date, or that special trip to a mountain cabin where you had a memorable weekend. It can be almost anything that has been a high point in your relationship.

For the ultimate gift pull off a surprise, four-day vacation trip. Arrange for a baby-sitter, if needed, purchase the plane tickets, arrange a hotel reservation, and be sure your spouse doesn't put a big conflict on the calendar. The day before the surprise trip, tell your spouse what to pack for a three- or four day trip. Only say two things: pack warm or cold, and casual or dressy. The anticipation will build and by the time you get on the plane it will be almost out of control. You cannot imagine the positive emotional response such a gift will generate.

I did this once when we were living in Corpus Christi, Texas, and I was able to keep the destination a secret until we changed planes in Dallas for the flight to Calgary, Canada. Vertis still smiles when we talk about that surprise trip. The positive emotional feedback from such a surprise will be worth every effort and dollar spent. (Well, I didn't say building a quality marriage was going to be without effort or cost, did I?)

That particular trip was a little costly, but as a mini-vacation it was worth every dollar. However, you don't have to come up with big bucks to do a lot of other surprises, even on special days when something is expected. Take Valentine's Day as an example. Yes, I've given candy—or at least I did until Vertis commented, "I'm dieting, and I won't be eating any more candy in this lifetime."

Of course, flowers and cards are sometimes appreciated, but, if you think about it, you get about 30 seconds of positive feedback—if that much—from those gifts. They are so expected that they're almost tossed aside. However, there are numerous ways to make those Valentine's Day gifts special. Instead of a card, write up some special thoughts about when you met your spouse, your first date, or maybe your wedding night. Or if you're a decent writer, compose a poem. Those thoughtful gifts will be remembered and probably kept for years.

However, being inventive on Valentine's Day can really give an emotional charge to a marriage. The following is a little something I did about 10-years ago for Valentine's Day. I decided to cook a gourmet—at least for a guy—dinner for Vertis. I know that sounds like a mess in the kitchen but the way I did it, it came out better than I ever thought it would. First, I sent her a printed invitation for dinner, and I noted the dress as "Formal" on the invitation. It perked Vertis's interest and she said, "Sound nice. Where are we going?"

Now the element of surprise came into play. "Somewhere you've never been," I answered. Well, that piqued her interest because we live in a town of 22,000, she's been to every restaurant in town, and I told her it would be in town.

It was a week before the night of the dinner, and I'd deliberately sent Vertis the invitation several days ahead to let her anticipate the gift. If you can have your spouse thinking about a gift days before it's given, you will increase the emotional impact of the gift—if you give the right gift. I had high hopes for the formal dinner I was going to prepare, but obviously there was some risk. What if I flopped as a chef? Or what if she was disappointed—expecting more? Remember, if you don't want your anticipated gift to fall in the "bad gift" category, you have to come through with a good gift. Never disappoint your spouse with an anticipated gift.

Of course, after sending the invitation and teasing Vertis it was time for me to make good on the formal dinner. I'm sure, if you wanted to spend mega-bucks, you could hire a catering service and let them do the whole spread. That would certainly be appreciated, but there's an easier way and a way to get the most emotions rise out of such a formal dinner.

I'd thought this out before I sent the invitation because I'm really not much of a cook—unless it's on a grill outside. But an outside grill was out because it was a formal occasion. This is what I came up with. One of Vertis's favorite dishes is soft-shell crab, so that became the entrée. I ordered it shipped overnight from the Crab House in Maryland. I decided on a spinach salad and steamed asparagus with Hollandaise Sauce. I could do this because the flash-frying of the soft-shell crabs was simple, as was the salad and asparagus, but the result were always predictable and very tasty.

Valentine's Day arrived and Vertis couldn't guess where we were going. She had eliminated every place in town in less than five minutes after she received the invitation. However, there was a large house in town, built in the 1920s that could be rented for receptions and wedding. I'd rented that house for the night. It had a full kitchen and by the time Valentine's rolled around I had everything in the kitchen ready to go.

That night I put on my tux at the office and at seven drove to my house to pick up Vertis. She was dressed to the nines, and could hardly contain her excitement. I drove across town to the house I'd rented, and she looked a little puzzled at first. We walked in to a warmly-lit, formal living room with soft music playing, and

I rushed into the kitchen to the freezer, where I'd already poured two glasses of champagne in red champagne glasses. We sipped our champagne and relaxed, and then I gave her a Valentine's card with a note about the first Valentine's Day we celebrated together. As we sat by the fireplace, we talked about our first Feb. 14 and what we had gotten each other. (My first gift to her was a pink sweater, and she gave me a red scarf—my favorite color.)

"Richard, I still have that sweater. I'll always keep it."

The evening was off to a great start, but being the chef was still to come, and I was nervous. After we finished our champagne, I said, "Come into the dining room. Dinner will be served in a few minutes."I could tell she was puzzled because it was obvious we were the only ones in the house. When she walked into the dining room, Vertis's face lit up.

That afternoon I'd cut about 50 bright-red camellia blossoms from a bush near our house, and I'd spread the red blossoms across the table. If I do say so myself, it made for a breathtaking setting. Actually, the camellia blossoms had been an afterthought, but a great one. Naturally, I'd already prepared the salads and in seconds I'd served them.

As we finished the salads I casually remarked, "I'm going to freshen up your champagne, and go in the kitchen and prepare dinner." I'll never forget that shocked looked on her face.

"Uh, wait, I'll go in and help you."

"No, I'm doing everything, and you just sit there and enjoy your champagne."

Later, Vertis, who is an excellent chef, told me it was the hardest thing she ever did to sit there while I prepared dinner. However, she did say the excitement and anticipation had her hands shaking. I'll be honest. I had everything ready, but I was nervous as a cat, because I had to steam the asparagus, fry the soft-shell crab, and heat up the Hollandaise Sauce all, at the same time while wearing a tux. Before I picked up Vertis I had put everything together, and when I served the salads, I'd turned the stove burners up to heat the cooking oil. I pulled it off and in less than 15-minutes, and then I placed dinner in front of a shocked wife and poured her a glass of Chardonnay. Dessert—already prepared (and purchased)—was in the freezer, and coffee followed.

I know that was a lot of work, but it was worth it. However, I do want to make one point before I leave this story. Vertis has never forgotten that night—and I haven't either. We reconnected during a busy week and that special night has been in both our memories. I know you might think Vertis was the one pleased and surprised, and that this Valentine's Day dinner was all for her pleasure. You'd be dead wrong if you thought that. Getting everything ready and preparing that dinner was the most fun I've had in years. Watching Vertis's enjoyment and surprise was worth all the effort I'd put into it. It was one of those special nights in a marriage that we bonded a little tighter, and during that special evening we relished each other's pleasure.

So let me sum up this gift-giving business: We live in a gift-giving society, and as those special days roll around it's almost mandatory to give your spouse something. But it doesn't have to be the same old boring thing—don't pay the water bill again. Take these mandatory occasions and make them memorable. I'm not the best at coming up with ways to make every one of these days special, so if I can come up with ideas that make these occasions memorable, so can you.

And finally, I know the illustrations above were from a male perspective, but, ladies, you're a lot more imaginative than I am, so let your creativity flow and you can accomplish much more than the little things I just mentioned.

Is gift-giving the panacea for a successful marriage? No, not by itself, but it is an integral part of a quality marriage, and, if you do it properly, your marriage will move up a notch toward that magic 95th percentile.

Premise # 10
Kids are one of the building blocks of a high-quality marriage

Kids

I'll bet you have friends who have some of the worst kids you've ever seen, and reflecting on those wild Indians, the idea that you'd bring kids into your marriage is about the last thing you'd want to do. So why bother with kids?

I guess, to explain why children matter, we must get back to the natural order of things, and dig deep into family relationships. The key is the family. Yes, you can have a family without having kids, but you can't have the multiple emotional actions and reactions that kids bring into the family.

A family is not complete without children—no matter what your sexual persuasion, religion, or anything else. I, personally, believe that a marriage with children experiences the fullness of a more complete family relationship.

My premise is simple: The positive emotional reactions that come by having kids in the family can move your marriage higher on the quality ladder. It boils down to a few points. These points can be summarized as love and fulfillment. Kids, just by being part of a family, bring more love and fulfillment into a marriage. Their contribution greatly outweighs the negatives. Look at it this way: Adding kids to a marriage gives you the opportunity to experience some very positive elements of life.

I've raised a couple of kids, and now I'm helping raise four grandkids, so I can tell you about both the heartaches followed by the mountain tops of joy that come from having kids in a family. So, in my opinion, if you want to get as much out of your marriage as possible, you'll have kids. Here are some other reasons why.

There's no doubt when kids are inserted into a marriage, things change. Ask any new parent. And it's not just the physical act of caring for the children, but the emotional makeup of the marriage becomes vastly different. When children are in a marriage the possible range of emotions immediately broadens, and things that never crossed your mind, all of a sudden, take on importance.

An ordinary high school soccer game may mean nothing to you, but if your child is playing, it becomes a must-see event, and if your kid kicks the winning goal, it's a moment of exhilaration that you could have never experienced if you hadn't brought children into your marriage.

But let's look deeper and consider our genetic makeup for just a minute. If we examine the most basic of human traits, we immediately find that procreating the species is right up there with eating and breathing. And the yearning to have, to raise, and to protect those kids is there whether we like it or not, and by not fulfilling those basic desires, you're leaving an emotional void in your life, that can only be filled by kids. There's no way to opt-out of those ingrained genetic traits. That's right, we all have a built-in drive to procreate. To have sex which will replenish the species, but it goes a lot farther than that. The same drive to procreate doesn't stop there. If it did we'd have millions of abandoned babies. There is something built into our system that makes us want to have, but not only to have, but to raise and nurture kids.

Granted, having children can put a damper on some activities, trips, and countless other things, and as kids go through puberty you'll want to pull your hair out. They can cause you untold misery in ways you can't even imagine—trust me on that one.

Well, if they're that many negatives, then there must be even more positive reasons for having children, or no one would ever have them. Of course, there are some very positive things about having kids in a marriage, or I wouldn't have written this chapter.

Kids have a special magic of their own in a marriage relationship, and probably the best part of that magic is the unexpected. Just as an unexpected gift can have an emotional positive effect in a marriage, the unexpected magic of an "A" in math can do the same. Having kids around guarantees your marriage will have thousands of those unexpected magic moments.

When you consider the positive emotional responses a child brings into a marriage, to survive marriage in the best way possible, kids need to be an integral part of your relationship. The interaction's of children with parents is one of the most positive and long-lasting of all human emotions.

I know there are hundreds of thousands of perfectly good satisfying marriages without kids, but, and this is a big but: Would those marriages be even better with kids? Will not having children keep those marriages from fulfilling their potential? Yes, I believe childless marriages, however wonderful they may be, can never reach their ultimate potential without the interactions of children. Those marriages can never experience some of the emotional qualities in their marriage that are available to couples with children, and yes, the bottom line is, kids enhance a marriage.

There is something, deep in our inner being, which makes life more desirable and pleasurable when children are around. We want to hold them, baby them, and take care of them. Many couples will tell you their child-rearing days were the happiest of their marriage, and they felt fulfilled in more ways than I could possible put in this book.

Of course, we all know couples who have struggled and fought with some really challenging kids and life was miserable for everyone around. Kids certainly aren't perfect little angels, and parents don't always do a good job of parenting. Granted, sometimes kids do disrupt a marriage. The reasons vary, but kid problems aren't endemic to all marriages. Those marriages are the exception. Most families have a warm, nurturing relationship in which their children are an integral part. These families would dismiss the idea that their family would be better off without kids. Let's face it; most of the marriages which have disruptive kids are just kids reacting to bad parenting. I believe it's the natural order of things to be around kids, and if that relationship is properly nurtured, you won't have bad kids, and those kids will add measurably to your marriage.

But just having kids won't help your marriage if the parents and the kids don't have a proper child/parent relationship. This is especially difficult in today's world, when kids are hooked on video games, their parents are off playing golf or bridge and dinner is a stop at a fast food place. So how do we insert kids into a marriage and make that marriage better? Well, making the marriage better is only one part of the equation. The equal part is how do we raise our children to be quality adults? The answer of course is to raise your kids in a manner that will produce quality adults, and if you do that, those quality kids will greatly enhance your marriage.

But, from the looks of a lot of marriages, there are many couples who are having trouble doing this. In these marriages, where kids are out of control, those marriages are anything but good-quality, and you could easily say in those marriages, kids are just in the way, or you might say, kids are making a bad marriage worse.

Well then, how should kids be handled in a marriage? First and foremost, the marriage partners must act like partners and share the responsibility for raising the kids and loving the kids, and in return receive the benefit of reciprocal love. If one parent is raising the kids, you can never have the quality child/parent relationship that can be reached in a child-rearing partnership. It works like this: Since over 80 percent of the mothers work today, it's real easy to toss aside the argument that mom should take care of the kids while dad works. If a man delegates the raising of the children to his wife, then they won't raise the best kids, and will miss one of the great benefits of marriage.

However, if we're talking about using kids as building blocks to survive marriage, then we should be sure those building blocks are handled properly. Kids who just grow up without love, discipline, or any structure in their lives are not going to be ideal building blocks for anyone's marriage, and they will have two strikes against them being good-quality adults.

Over the years I've watched parents try to rear kids in every possible way. Some parents give their children everything they want except one item—their time. In today's hectic world one of the most valuable assets—and one that is the most difficult to attain—is time. All of the positive features we can name will never happen without parents devoting time to the kids. Yes, you can always have a list of things that take priority over your family and sometimes, just to keep bread on the table, you have to put your work first. However, most of the time giving your kid priority time will not affect your job. Anything on that list that comes ahead of family must be carefully scrutinized and most of the time a close examination will result in lowering that non-family priority.

If we do give our kids the time they need, usually, that will, by itself, provide the necessary upbringing they require.

Everyone's goal is to raise children to be responsible, successful adults, but unless we devote quality time to them, we can't possibly expect them to be the adults we want them to be. However, kids need not only a parent who will be there and do things with them, but also a parent who will serve as an example. You can't get by with "Don't do as I do; do as I say." Unless the parents are positive role models, the kids have two strikes against them. In a family relationship it is impossible to disguise your true nature, and if your marriage is struggling the kids will know it.

Your kids will see through every façade you put up—every time. A good-quality marriage and kids are linked together in so many ways that it is impossible to list them. It's trite to say, "You can't have one without the other." I just think open honesty in child/parent relationships and in a spousal relationship is critical if you want to have quality. Without basic honesty, that's impossible.

It all comes down to honest relationships within the family unit. If we want kids who contribute to the well-being of our family, and if we want kids that will add to the joy of family life, then we must have a positive, uplifting honest marriage that shows outward love to every member of the family. If kids feel love is present between parents, and naturally to them, they will most likely respond in love.

However, I have known many couples, who were in the midst of serious marriage problems, and decided to have kids in order to try and save the marriage. Obviously, just the basic idea that bringing more stress into a marriage is a positive is ludicrous. Kids can move the marriage relationship up to another level, but only if that relationship is already strong, positive and growing. The odds are stacked against you if you think bringing kids into a shaky marriage will save it.

The more likely scenario is that the addition of kids will cause the final destruction of that marriage. Then not only will you be divorced, but the kids will be pulled between parents, and what should have been a building block to a better marriage will become a stumbling block to a new life.

So, consider your current relationship before you bring kids into your marriage. If you have a warm, loving marriage, kids will make it better, but they probably won't help a shaky one.

But bringing kids into a marriage is more than filling a void. It's the satisfaction and enjoyment within the family that's enhanced by sharing joy with other family members. It can be as simple as feeling a surge of pride when your 8-year-old catches a fly ball, or when your daughter spells a word right in a spelling bee.

Sharing happiness and joy with kids will build up your marriage and give you more of a long-term positive affect than you would have had without kids. When you share the joy of your children, you are emotionally strengthening the bond with your mate. You are sharing a responsibility, and your pride and joy is a common link to making your marriage better.

Kids have problems and cause problems, just as we all do, but when we balance the pleasure which they bring into a marriage, by allowing you to share their lives, the problems are usually much less of a factor. A can be marriage more uplifting and pleasing, even with the problems kids bring into it, than a marriage without them.

However, I know many couples who would love to have children, but because of some reproductive problem in one or both marriage partners, they can't. What can these married couple do? Well, the easy answer is to do what we did—adopt. Yes, we tried for seven-years without success and never did understand why Vertis couldn't get pregnant. We adopted both of our children from the Texas Welfare Department, and we have never regretted it.

In today's world there are literally millions of homeless children who would make wonderful additions to any marriage. I speak from experience when I say to seek out an adoption agency, or go through one of the many overseas programs that place kids. There's a child out there somewhere who would make a meaningful improvement to your marriage. Adopt, if you can't have children. I promise you won't regret the move.

But there's another reason to have kids, and as far as I'm concerned, at this stage in my life, it's a huge plus. A marriage without children means you won't have grandchildren. A lot of parents complain about kids, but very few ever complain about their grandkids. Grandchildren are your kids all over again, and you have the best part of raising them. You get all the joy out of having them come to see you, watching them play in sports or perform, and just be around them, and then they go home to mom and dad for the discipline, feeding, and yes, diaper- changing. It's absolutely the best of both worlds.

You can spoil them, talk baby talk to them, feed them (occasionally) the junkest fast food imaginable and then, give them a hug, and send them back to their parents. What could be a better arrangement? In my opinion, grandkids in a quality marriage substantially adds to the enjoyment of life. Not only do kids improve a marriage, but grandkids give it an additional boost.

Now to the final reason to have kids, and this almost seems self-serving. I know many older adults who have ended up needing care during the very last years of life. Almost all elderly adults reach a time where they need either mental or physical help—usually both. In the natural order of things, the children of those elderly adults provide the help in this stage of life just as the adults provided care for the kids when they were young.

I know when you're trying to survive marriage, worrying about old age is about the last thing you want to do, but life can be exact and cruel for senior adults. We will all need assistance sometime in the late stages of our life. If we don't have our children to assist us, who will?

So, what's the bottom line? It's very simple. Kids will further enhance a positive emotional relationship. If you and your spouse bring kids into your marriage and handle them properly, kids will add to the marriage in a very meaningful way.

I can assure you that my children and grandchildren have immeasurably increased the joy in our marriage, and I can't imagine not having them. So, as you build a solid, good-quality marriage, add kids to the mix. They are just one more building block to reach the top-quality marriage we would all like to have. You won't be sorry, because those kids will give you an incalculable amount of joy and satisfaction. I promise.

Premise # 11

A marriage lived together is a prerequisite to a top-quality marriage

Together

This chapter is aimed at trying to revive those marriages that are marriages in name only. You probably have some in your neighborhood. They're the couples who live in the same house and occasionally interact to make love, but other than that, they live almost separate lives. They are seemingly getting along fine doing their own thing. But are they?

If you knew the interworking of their marriage, would you gasp at how void of affection and interaction it is? Would their marriage be better if they interacted more? Sure it would, and that's the focus of this chapter.

The best quality marriage and the best life possible is one where couples do as much as possible—together. I know that sounds as if it's a tall order to fill, especially to all those couples who have been doing their own thing for years. If your idea of a marriage is to occasionally show up to eat a meal together and have sex, this chapter is going to be a speed bump for you.

Before we get into the whys of togetherness, let's consider the alternative, which I call, "Marriage-Lite." This is a marriage where the couples don't even physically sleep together. Each has a separate set of friends, and they live essentially two unrelated lives. Their recreation is separate, as is most of their free time on weekends. You might say they're married in name only. They exhibit very few of the traits of a married couple, much less a happily married couple. It's barely a step up from dating.

A lot of these couples might say they have more freedom living in that manner, that it works for them, or that too much togetherness is not right for them. "If we're around each other too much, we start getting on each other's nerves." Have you heard that statement before? Sure you have. Many of these couples go about life seemingly enjoying themselves, and to the average person their marriage is fine. But could it be better? Yes, I think it could be, and not just incrementally better. Here's why.

To understand why the "Marriage-Lite" plan isn't a positive way to increase the emotional ties that make a good marriage, consider this simple fact: Absence does not make the heart grow fonder. No matter what the old proverb says. Absence always results in the marriage partners becoming less intimate. Can you imagine a close intimate relationship with someone you rarely see? Of course not.

That's the real reason why togetherness works. Instead of drawing apart because you're separated most of the time, you become more and more emotionally bound. Maybe your marriage is on the rocks, or at least it's not what it could be and you're looking for some answers. Sometimes we try to solve a problem by proposing the most complicated solution when the answer is simple. Could it be as simple as the fact that you're not doing enough together? Let me expand on that subject, because that's the crux of this chapter.

Let's back up for a minute. The goal for every marriage partner, or for every individual for that matter, should be to live the best life possible—in every way. I contend that to have a marriage partnership of the highest quality, a couple should strive to have similar likes and dislikes. If marriage partners enjoy the same things, it stands to reason that they will naturally gravitate to do these things together—and very simply build up emotional ties by just being together. If they do this, then they'll have a better chance of living the best life possible by making togetherness a primary component of their marriage.

Remember this: For your marriage to achieve the level of togetherness that will strengthen your marriage substantially, the marriage partners must agree that doing things together is a positive. But not only must they agree, but they also must actually do as many things together on a daily basis as possible. It can't be hit and miss and or just a matter of doing something together just on special occasions.

Togetherness will move your relationship to a higher plateau only if there is a continued, daily, concentrated effort to do as many things together as possible. Consider just for a moment how simple this really is. Just being together in a pleasant atmosphere, where a couple experiences pleasure, is a building block to a better marriage relationship. Something as simple as going to the movies or out to dinner can improve the emotional ties that bind a marriage together.

However, don't believe for a minute that an occasional movie or dinner will substantially improve your marriage. To really get the most out of this premise, it will take a lot more than an occasional movie or dinner to get the maximum emotional benefit from doing things together.

Now let's look a little deeper into this idea of togetherness, because there are pros and cons in every relationship or even business decision. Everything you do has consequences. Many times those consequence are subtle, but they are always there. It's the same situation when we analyze the benefits gained in a marriage simply by doing things together.

I've looked into the seemingly simple statement—doing things together—and I'll be honest, I was amazed at the benefits and shocked at the few negatives. For a few minutes consider the positive benefits of being with someone you love, or on the other hand, doing something else away from them. Then make a list of the positive times you spent with your spouse and a second list of the things you did away from your spouse. If your list of negatives greater than your positives, you have some serious relationship problems. Lovers, because of their very nature want to be together. It's that simple. Togetherness equals more affection.

Let me give you an example in my marriage of how a rather unusual act of togetherness works to buildup emotional ties. We bathe together—every morning. Now I know you're shaking your head, but hear me out. First of all we don't have a conventional bathtub. Our tub is a variety called a Roman Tub. It's 6 feet long and around 5 feet wide—plenty of room for two people. I know this might sound like something a newlywed couple might do, but let me tell you why it works for us. It's part of our daily routine just as much as working out or going for a Coke at 10 o'clock. We return from our morning workout around seven and after breakfast we head for our bathroom to clean up and get ready for work.

Our morning bath is something I look forward to, but not just because I like bathing with a gorgeous blonde. No, it a lot more than that. It's a time to lean back and relax in warm water while we discuss the day ahead. There's something about the intimacy of being in a relaxed, pleasant atmosphere for 15-minutes or so that gets the day off to a great start. Sometimes we'll talk about having friends over for dinner. Other times we'll discuss upcoming vacations or any one of a hundred ordinary things that come up between married couples.

And yes, bathing with an attractive person of the opposite sex does occasionally cause an interest in sex. So, as unusual as it may seem, our bathing together is just a natural part of the togetherness we have as a couple. And it's environmentally sound—think of all the water we're saving by bathing together.

I know I'm repeating myself, but doing thing together and having common interests are good for a marriage. Not only are they good, they always lead to a closeness that is hard to define. That's because of the intertwined personal relationships, which have developed as a result of simply doing things together.

I'm not trying to smother you into a boring, uncomfortable relationship where you're dreading what the next day or night will bring with your spouse. Just the opposite. If your idea of a good-quality marriage is working toward a deep, committed relationship, then being with the marriage partner will be just the opposite from boring. You'll look forward to those times you're together and, when you miss sharing something, the first thing you'll do is tell your spouse what he or she missed.

The best way to tell if your marriage relationship has emotional togetherness is to gauge how you feel when you are away from your partner for a day or two. If you have a deep sense of missing that person, and if you mentally count the days until you're back together again, then you have a togetherness that has emotionally bonded you. Part of the quality marriage we're striving for is within your grasp.

However, as many marriages mature, sometimes ingrained habits gradually separate the couple to the point where doing things together seems far-fetched. Let's take a look at two imaginary partners who have let that happen.

Let's say the wife plays bridge most days, then works on her FaceBook page until bedtime and then reads until she falls asleep. She only calls her husband at work if there's an emergency, and they eat dinner together only once a week.

Her husband is a driven workaholic who leaves for work before his wife gets up, works late, rarely takes a vacation, and never calls his wife. Most afternoons he stops at a bar on the way home from work, missing dinner on a regular basis. They have sex no more than once a week and it's not particularly fulfilling for either of them. Their friends think they have a very successful marriage.

Now, let's look at the way this marriage is structured. It's similar to a lot of marriages where two individuals live in the same house and sometimes take vacations together, but outside of an occasional night out to a good restaurant, they rarely do things together. And the night out at the good restaurant is often a silent indictment of how sick their marriage really is. That night out is a guilt night, and when the couple sits down and waits to order they have almost nothing to say to each other. Their interests are so removed that conversation is nonexistent.

These couples may say they don't have anything in common to talk about, but a close examination of their marriage would show they have many areas of mutual enjoyment. If that's the case, and if the two are serious about wanting to move their relationship to a better level, then there's hope.

First, let's take a long-term look at this marriage. Where will it be in 10, 15, or 20 years? Statistics tell us at least half of the couples in similar marriages will have divorced. The other half will still be struggling along, maybe staying together for the kids, and a third of these surviving couples will have or are having an affair. Not exactly the ideal marriage relationship to strive for. Can marriages of this nature be saved?

Not unless the marriage partners commit to a complete change in their lifestyle. They can stay legally married, but that—in my opinion—is even worse than divorce. This couple needs to do many things. First, let's look at the wife. The biggest problem I see is her lack of quality time and infrequent contacts during the day with her husband. That's a sure-fire marriage killer, and here's why.

Marriage couples that seem to have successful marriages but take completely different tracks when it came to entertainment and recreation, are usually creating an illusion. A close look at their marriage would reveal something less than a good-quality relationship. Sure, it's inherent in human nature that men—who have their testosterone boiling in their 20s—are going to be more aggressive in their pursuit of recreation, but does this mean that women can't be involved? Of course not, but maybe not in the direct way a man might be.

Consider this: Most outdoor activities are not one-dimensional. In other words, while shooting ducks may seem to be the whole idea of a duck hunt for one partner, the spouse might see a duck hunt as a trip into a natural setting and a chance to enjoy the outdoor scenery and relish stopping by a nice restaurant for lunch on the way home. I think you get the point.

However, it's certainly not far-fetched to think both marriage partners would be interested in actually shooing ducks. I do know a lot of couples who duck hunt together, and the wives frequently come back with more ducks! It can work, but it takes flexibility and determination when the recreational activity is not exactly your cup of tea.

But let's get back to the premise of this chapter: Is a "togetherness" marriage living the best quality life possible? Or is that marriage idea one for the birds? How about the long-term potential? Actually, if we consider the long-term relationship issues, the benefits that accrue to a close, almost inseparable couple are remarkable. Instead of gradually growing apart, the couple will become closer, and as they do more things together, they will become more emotionally bonded. Closer, emotionally bonded couples are always happier.

I know a couple who are both 94, and they now only have themselves to keep each other company. What if they had lived

Marriage-Lite for all those years? I imagine that old age is much harder to go through if you don't have a close companion to share it with you. But if you think working for a togetherness marriage is just for old-age companionship, you're missing the whole point. The idea is to create a relationship and maintain it for as long as you can.

If our goal is to reach a plateau relationship where the maximum marriage benefits are enjoyed for as long as possible, then you must have a togetherness marriage, because it is impossible for a "separate" marriage to ever reach that level. If you get nothing else from this book, take this to heart: You can never have the best relationship possible, if you have a separate marriage. The closer your relationship is, the better quality it becomes.

Naturally, there are all stages of separation or togetherness in a marriage, and in every marriage the partners should evaluate how far away they are from the emotional closeness that nurtures a good marriage. And if they need to take steps to enhance that relationship, the partners should introduce more togetherness.

So, if you want to settle for something less than the best, go ahead and have Marriage-Lite. But, if your goal is to be best friends and know everything about your partner, and bond deeply in a loving, friendship relationship—till death do you part—forget the separate marriage and look for ways to stay close. You can't possible reach the marriage plateau I'm talking about by living two separate lives. And you'll never live the best life you could live—and that's a fact.

Of course, by now you've read a lot of this book, and you know I think if you don't bond emotionally, you will miss the better part of marriage. But this chapter is not solely for couples who go to the extreme in living apart; it's also directed at those who give lip service to living together, but when they put their priorities down on paper, togetherness is usually pushed to the bottom of the list. It won't work unless togetherness is a priority in every aspect of your marriage.

There are many way you can build on your relationship. If you do want to build a long and satisfying marriage that continues to grow over the years, then cultivate common interests. I've heard couples say, "We have absolutely nothing in common." Well, surely these couples who espouse that didn't get married solely for sex. The more likely scenario is that when they were dating and first married there were numerous things they did together. Now after years of marriage they have drifted apart and don't really don't have much in common but sex. (And I'll bet the sex isn't much to brag about either.)

Togetherness depends upon the couple, not the individual. There needs to be a willingness to change by both marriage partners—to where they become more of a couple rather that two people who happen to live together. One partner can't possibly be happy having to put up with someone who cares absolutely only about his or her own interests. Let me give you an example of how compatibility and togetherness is supposed to work. A few years ago a female friend of mine began to date a man she'd met through a mutual friend. They fell in love and were married six months later. The husband was, and still is, an avid bridge player and golfer, and the wife loves to go out to dinner and travel. Neither marriage partner seemed to have any interest in doing what the other thought of as recreation. It was a bumpy relationship for a while, but only a short while. The wife decided that if their marriage was going to make it, she would have to make some concessions. She took up golf and learned to play bridge. It was difficult for her to master a card game and sport that she knew nothing about but she did. And, as the months passed, their marriage relationship began to change. He began to respond by traveling and dining out more. Today, they travel, play golf and bridge and dine at great restaurants. As a result of marriage partners co-operating, the emotional bonds that hold their marriage together strengthened appreciably. They have a great marriage.

Of course, that's simplifying a complex situation, but it makes a point. First, the wife made a positive move. Even though she didn't have any interest in either golf or bridge, she tackled both with enthusiasm. The result surprised even her. She actually learned to love both and has excelled. The bonding with her husband has strengthened their marriage dramatically. Did he appreciate her commitment? Yes, in a most positive way. And as he responded, she was able to see him change his habits and desires. As a result, they strengthened their emotional bonds.

The whole point of togetherness is not to be physically involved in everything your spouse does. Yes, it can work that way, but real togetherness is more mental than physical. Marriages are not shaped by the physical nearly as much as they are by emotional bonding. That's right, the mental part of togetherness comes when you share something, and that togetherness creates a positive emotional bonding. A truly happy couple can enjoy the simplest things, and because they have bonded emotionally, being together and doing almost anything together is perceived by them as enjoyable and pleasurable.

Think back to when you were dating, and you went to everything from revivals to dance recitals just to be with the one you were pursuing. And did you enjoy yourself? Well, maybe not the event, but in your mind you came away with a pleasurable experience because it was with the one you cared about. Marriage is the same way only more so. When you were dating, it was an hour or two here and there, and you constantly thought of those times. Now you're married and that moves the peg up to a new level, because now you can be together daily and for hours at a time. This is why togetherness is such a great opportunity to enhance your marriage. If your attitude is right, every minute of togetherness cements that emotional bond a little tighter and moves you toward that ultimate marriage.

Remember, you can't have the best life possible if you don't excel in togetherness.

Premise # 12

Having a good-quality spiritual life is a building block to a great marriage

Be Spiritual

Let me put it right up front: I'm a Christian, a Southern Baptist, but a very liberal Southern Baptist. I've been a Sunday School Teacher and Adult Choir Member for decades. As I look back on those years when I served in my church, I am convinced that those years of service made a meaningful improvement in my marriage—and of course my overall life. I'm still teaching Adult Sunday School and singing in the church choir—and still reaping the benefits from being spiritual.

In my mind, a spiritual connection shared by spouses is a critical part of a foundation for a great marriage and a top-quality life. Spirituality can't be emphasized enough because it plays such an important part in life. Actually, there are reams of polls and studies that confirm the positive aspect of being spiritual. There's even one that says the sexual experience is better if a couple is spiritual. So, yes, I'm spiritual, and so is Vertis. In fact her father was a Baptist preacher. She's what I call a "Deep-water Baptist."

With that background, let me give you my take on being spiritual. Yes, I know there are millions, maybe billions, of people around the world who will tell you they're spiritual, and they're not Christians. Maybe they are spiritual, I'm not a judge of whether someone is spiritual or not. I can only tell you what has worked in my own life.

But let's answer the question of why being spiritual together helps build a top-quality life, and not get hung up on who is and who isn't spiritual. The question is "Will being spiritual help you survive marriage and live the best life possible?" And if it will, how and why?

There have been reams of studies that have examined how being spiritual can improve your quality of life. After all, our basic premise for writing this book is to put forth a recipe for living the best life possible, and you know by now I'm convinced that the best life possible is a married life with the couple functioning almost as one, to enjoy and to get as much pleasure out of life as possible—and being spiritual is part of the mix.

As I thought about the contributing factors that would come into play to help a couple reach a high-quality marriage plateau of marriage few ever attain, the idea of being spiritual together was something I'd taken for granted. Then it occurred to me that just because Vertis and I have always enjoyed a spiritual relationship, it would be foolish to assume everyone did. That brought me to the point where I began to look closely into the connections among contentment, joy, pleasure, peace and numerous other attributes of a quality life, as they relate to spirituality.

There are numerous studies showing that Christian married couples live longer, have more satisfying sex lives, and experience a life full of a myriad of other factors that equal a quality life. A short answer to all of those studies is that individuals who are spiritual have more fulfilling lives. Now let's look at how being spiritual can improve your married life. First, be spiritual—together. Why together? Well, the Apostle Paul touched on the subject in the first century. "Be not unequally yoked together…" Paul was writing about Christians who were contemplating marriage with non-believers—probably Christian Jews marrying non-believing Greeks.

The idea of being "unequally yoked" is an agriculture expression that referrers to yoking a team of oxen together. A team can't pull effectively if one ox is bigger, stronger, or not of the same temperament as the other. A farmer will carefully select his team and match the oxen. It's easy to understand why—they are more productive when equally yoked.

Marriage and life are not exactly like a team of oxen, but there are similarities. Sometimes being unequally yoked can mean that each partner comes from vastly different backgrounds, and that can be a problem (but we won't go into to that situation here). In this chapter I'm only going to cover the spiritual part of being unequally yoked.

In a marriage there will always be times when spirituality is involved. It may be when a tragedy or a major illness strikes someone in the immediate family. The impact of that event will be felt differently by a spiritual member of the family versus the non-spiritual person. Life events such as the ones mentioned above require a particular understanding and emotional resolve in order for the couple to survive and get through it. Can being spiritual help a marriage during these times? Let me give you an example of how a spiritual marriage reacted to a grave illness and how a non-spiritual person reacted.

Early in our marriage we became close friends with a young man in his early 20s. He was a not spiritual in the least, but he was our good friend and we enjoyed his company. The crisis in his life came when he went to the doctor to be examined because of a growing lump under his arm. It was horrible news—cancer. He was devastated, and after receiving the news he came by our house just to be with friends. It was heartbreaking.

After talking with him for several hours, then praying for him, he was tearful and got up to leave. I'll never forget that moment. We walked him to the door, hugged him, and Vertis said, "Here Doug, I want you to have this." She handed Doug her personal Bible. He was surprised, but he took it and, for a long minute, just stared at the Bible. Then, as tears streamed down his face, he said. "I wish I had your faith to get through this. I feel so empty." It was a haunting refrain that I've had in my mind for decades. The young man desperately needed something to get him though an emotional and stressful time in his life. He wanted to be spiritual. He needed to be spiritual.

That's one of the primary reasons I feel a couple should have a positive spiritual life. It's an uplifting experience during the good times of life and it actually enhances the enjoyment of some of the pleasurable moments a couple can share together. And, yes, it's a solace and undergirds us when we traverse the hard times of life.

But let's look a little deeper into the matter. Being unequally yoked doesn't always mean one partner is a Christian and the other is not. It can mean they are members of different denominations, or maybe they espouse different religions. Either way, problems will usually crop up, and solving spiritual problems can be one of the most vexing situations a marriage can encounter.

I've watched couples try to raise children in families where they're pulled between religions. It almost never works to the benefit of the kids. Many times, one parent will demand the children be raised under his or her spiritual guidelines, even when the other parent objects strenuously. If a conflict in spirituality is an integral part of a marriage, that couple will never reach the marriage plateau that they're striving for. It will be a thorn in the marriage for as long as the difference persists, and it will, without question, degrade their overall quality of life.

Therefore, I caution those of you who are planning to marry to settle the religious or spiritual issues before marriage. In the Christian faith, which is the more likely scenario with Americans, it's usually different denominations. The best results may come from a compromise—not attending either spouse's church. That way, both start at essentially the same level in a new church and the partners can grow together spiritually.

However, don't assume that if both individuals are Christians they will mature spiritually at the same speed. This problem occurs more than you might imagine. Vertis and I have been friends with two couples, both of whom were regular church attendees. When they married, they continued to be active in their church for a number of years. Then, one of the partners in each marriage began to spend many extra hours in Bible study, prayer, and a daily Bible study group. That, by itself, is fairly common in a marriage, and usually isn't a problem. However, these two couples slowly became unequally yoked, spiritually. One partner's accelerated spiritual growth created tension in both marriages, until in one of the marriages, the couple divorced.

According to the spouse that wasn't the deep spiritual seeker, the spirituality gap became a point of contention. Soon it was an open wound that darkened everything from sex life to their social life. After the one couple divorced, the partners went through a time where they reflected back on what had been a positive marriage, and—although I'm not privy to confidential conversations—they seemed to have resolved their spiritually problems, because they remarried.

Now, let's sum up spirituality as it effects marriage: A marriage that is underpinned by a common spiritual belief is stronger than one that's not. The simple reasoning behind this statement focuses on the emotional bond that is so important in marriage. A common faith ensures a stronger bond. Spirituality brings the couple together in times of trials, and the enjoyment of happy occasions is intensified by having a spiritual dimension. If only one partner is spiritual, then the marriage will never reach its potential.

Don't get me wrong, I'm not saying you can't have a decent marriage if you are of different faiths. You may be compatible and love each other enough to compensate. However, I'm putting forth the ideal. If the same couple has spirituality in common, they can reach a higher plane of marriage. The spiritual bonding will knit an emotional framework that will make their marriage stronger, and what had been a good marriage can build toward greatness.

Spirituality in a marriage is also one of the glues that binds two individuals into one and makes the trauma of life bearable. Of course, spirituality is no stranger to most marriages, but having a true bond of spirituality is. Let me explain my viewpoint: There is something basic and deep within the human soul that expresses itself in a need to interact with a supreme being, to relate in some way to God. As far as we can look back in recorded history, we see mankind worshiping and building temples or other structures to some god. Of course, those temples aren't to the same god, but the intent is the same. Man has an inner desire to worship. If a couple uses that inherent desire to worship as a way to increase the intimacy and togetherness in a marriage, it will appreciably enhance their lives.

Numerous studies have shown that we are more content and basically happier when we are involved in organized religion. It's not only the spiritual aspect of being in an organized religion, it's the social. Many couples end up making close friends in their church congregation and some individuals further their involvement in the church service by teaching Sunday School or singing in the choir. I'm not trying to convert anyone, but it's a fact: Being involved together in a religious service is a building block of a successful marriage.

However, spiritually in a marriage doesn't always work out perfectly. I know many of us have seen marriages that didn't improve when a couple became more spiritual. In fact conflicts within their spirituality actually made their lives worse. Because of a person's deep convictions, problems of a spiritual nature can be very difficult to overcome. When that happens it's not time to throw in the towel, but it is time to begin major repairs on that marriage. The very nature of spirituality is love, and if a couple can remove the bitterness from a spiritual conflict and concentrate on the positive aspects of their faith, they'll overcome these problems. A lot of the time spiritual conflicts will be caused by different methods of worship. Traditions in the Christian community vary greatly, and what would shock one churchgoer would be just a normal service for someone else.

However, if Christians focus on the primary aspect of Christianity, the belief in Christ and His love, they'll find out that they have the basic foundation of spirituality in common. A focus on the commonality of faith can smooth over many conflicts. But it takes flexibility and compromise to bring about a positive result.

Spirituality is in this book because we need to use every avenue possible to make marriage work. To fix a broken or wounded marriage, and improve your life, it may take a multiple focus on several areas of conflict. That's where being spiritual, and part of an organized religion, is important. It's another tool to enhance and sometimes repair broken or bent relationships.

To better understand why spirituality helps, let's analyze the basic aspect of religion. Most, if not all, religions require participation in some sort of service, and many offer music, meditation, and other enhancements to worship. In addition, just the emotional intimacy created when marriage partners come together to worship is a very strong positive experience. The bumper sticker that says, "The family that prays together, stays together," has validity.

But—and here's a key—don't just stick your toe in the water, so to speak. That doesn't mean you need to be jumping pews, but full involvement by both parties is the best way to receive the full benefit from religion. The very act of having a daily prayer together is an intimate moment that will build up the strength and sustainability of a marriage. Not only that, but it increases the pleasure of everyday life situations. The baptism of a grandchild, for example, means so much more to a couple who share spirituality together, and teaching a young child the basic tenants of your faith is a very rewarding experience.

In any long marriage there will be times when the solace of a shared religion will be not only comforting, but will bind that marriage tighter, and the couple will come out of those situations with a closer bond than before the crisis occurred. After all, every marriage that lasts for any decent time is going to have life problems and family emergencies to contend with.

Having the bulwark of religion to steady a marriage is sometimes the difference in seeing a marriage disintegrate because of a family tragedy, or to come out of that tragedy stronger. After all, we can't expect to have a marriage or life where the couple is always happy. It's not possible. There are times when tragedy strikes a family and that marriage is strained and sometimes even pulled apart. Many times it's because one individual is religious and the other is not. Therefore, it certainly makes sense to make worship and attending religious services together a part of you weekly life.

My recommendation is to start your day off (or end your day) with several minutes of quiet time, and then read something you can meditate on. After a few minutes, have a time of silent prayer, or if your relationship is open enough, have prayer with your wife or husband and speak those prayers audibly; one spouse could pray one day and the other the next. And somewhere in that prayer—pray for each other. Try it and you'll find there is something about someone actually praying for you, by name, which is comforting and soothing. It's also hard to be angry with someone who is praying for you.

Another benefit to being spiritual is that you'll develop friends who have similar religious beliefs, assuming you attend service where other believers of your faith worship. The strength that these friends will give you during times of stress and tragedy will help carry you through the healing process, and in doing so bring you out of your problems stronger and more committed than you were before the problem.

Religion can also be a healer when marriage rifts occur. If you believe there is a perfect marriage waiting for you, even if you're perfect in every way mentioned in this book, you're kidding yourself. We're human and we have weaknesses and those weakness create disagreements—sometimes extremely vocal ones. Looking back on our marriage, I can tell you from firsthand experience that 95 percent of these little arguments have been about things that were incidental to our marriage.

In the early years of our marriage, if we got into a bad disagreement on a Friday, we didn't fully make up until Sunday. However, if we happen to get into an argument on Sunday morning, by the time we leave church, we're over it. It's hard to pray and worship when you're not happy with your spouse. I can tell you right now, without any doubt, being spiritual dissipates most arguments.

Another benefit from attending religious services comes with learning the tenants of the religion. Most teach love of your fellow man and, of course, your spouse falls right into that category. But it's a lot more than that. Our entire set of Judeo-Christian laws, which are the foundation of our morality, are based on tenants set out by our faith. The study and practice of these tenants will not only enhance your feeling for your spouse, but will make you a better citizen and, consequently, a better life partner.

Survey after survey has found that regular attendees of religious services have stronger marriages, live longer, and yes, even have a better sex life. So vow to make what has been ingrained in mankind since creation—a desire to worship—as part of the way you'll develop a high-quality life. Very simply put: A spiritual marriage is worth surviving because it gives one a better, more enjoyable life.

So the bottom line to being spiritual in your marriage is that you'll have fewer negative thoughts about your spouse, and therefore become closer and have a more fulfilling marriage. And spirituality will become a building block to the best life possible

It's one more step to reaching the 95th percentile.

Premise # 13
To have a top-quality marriage you must compromise

Compromise

All of us have seen marriages with serious problems. But I've found out that many times a closer examination of these marriages usually finds that the problems are seemingly insignificant. An outside view of those marriages usually reveals that the marriage partners are intransigent in their disagreement. They haven't learned one of the primary tenants that make a good marriage: being flexible and willing to compromise. In other words, ignore the little snide remarks and don't be mad for days when you concede a point or lose an argument. Or actually worse, don't finish the argument—let it simmer for days and days—as you make everyone in the house miserable. A rigid, inflexible attitude is a sure recipe for a sub-par marriage.

We all have bad days, and when we do it's really easy to snap and argue at the drop of a hat. To make matters worse, because we're in such a rotten mood, getting over that little squabble is much harder to do. Over the years I've learned to be especially on guard when things—like a dry hole—have just smacked me in the face. (I'm an oil and gas exploration geologist.)

I have a tendency to take my bad day out on everybody I come in contact with—especially Vertis. Most of the time she'll understand, and we can smooth over a catty remark, or something that's so insignificant that the next day we'd laugh about arguing over it. However, there are days when we come in from work ready to fight—not physically, of course—at the slightest word.

And it doesn't take much to set us off. We're an emotional couple and our "little" arguments can go from zero to 60 in seconds. Those are the days we have to let common sense overcome our emotions.

However, let me make myself clear on the subject: I'm not saying don't ever argue or get into verbal fights. That's not possible. The problem is not the argument or the fight or whatever you want to call those times when couples disagree. It's the unbending, rigid attitude of one or both of the marriage partners. Disagreements by themselves aren't going to cripple a marriage and reduce your quality of life, but inflexibility and just plain old hard-headedness will certainly lower the quality of your marriage and, naturally, your life.

Early in our marriage we would easily carry those little disagreements into the next day and sometimes longer. We've got over that. Today we can still go from zero to 60 in seconds, but we don't stay there long. No matter who fired the first shot, one of us will calm down enough to give the other a hug and say something like, "This is one of the dumbest fights we've had in a long time." That will usually break the ice, and we'll smile and maybe even laugh.

You know, as simple as that sounds, it's one of the keys to keeping a marriage upright. Simmering fights that go on for days slowly erode even the strongest marriages and make for a degraded quality of life. Here are two rules. One: Don't sweat the small stuff—and realize most of the stuff is small stuff. Two: Forgive quickly, and forget.

In our marriage forgetting is sometimes our biggest problem, and we have to hold ourselves to keep from reliving some of the choicest shots of the fight. If a couple can shortcut the many insignificant arguments that are common to every marriage, and completely forget them—for good—these disagreements will not chip away at the emotional bonds of the marriage, but will allow the couple more quality time together, which will enhance the marriage.

I know you might think I'm placing too much attention on little insignificant arguments, but remember this: A marriage that becomes argumentative and stays that way—even if the issues are minor—quickly moves down on quality. It's important to have a balanced marriage, though by being balanced I don't mean being a doormat and putting up with everything that is thrown at you.

Vertis and I are two headstrong individuals, and the idea that one of us would be milquetoast in an argument is laughable. A marriage where one partner dominates the other won't ever be the best it can be, and it certainly won't allow you to live the best life possible. That marriage can never be a true partnership. Spouses should have an open discussion about everything that has to do with their relationship, and each marriage partner's opinion should carry the same weight.

But for a moment let's continue to discuss the partnership idea in marriage as it pertains to disagreements. No one wants to be married to a doormat, and unless your marriage is relatively equal in strength, you can't have the quality life you're seeking. Can you imagine your wife saying, "It okay with me, darling, if you go to Boy's Town." (For non-Texans, that's the section of Mexican border towns with prostitutes.)

I don't know about you, but I wouldn't want to be married to a woman without a backbone—or, even worse, a man without one. While there is no place in a partnership marriage for a dominant partner, there's no place for a submissive one either. Vertis has never been shy about speaking her mind (that's sure an understatement) and I think more of her for it.

But back to partnership discussions, which many times turn out to be arguments. I can guarantee you that even the best marriages there will be arguments, and unless you're married to a real dud, you should lose as many arguments as you win. And for God's sake, remember this, if you lose hands-down, don't fold up and pout, but put the argument behind you and move on. Don't let losing an insignificant argument cut into your quality time with your spouse. Never go to bed with an unresolved argument. Actually, in real life, since most arguments are draws, you need to quickly put them behind you, after they've been thrashed out sufficiently. Then kiss and makeup and don't do it half-heartedly. There's nothing worse than an under-the-scenes, simmering fuss.

But back to the inevitable: Couples are going to argue. Yes, it's going to happen. Unless you really are married to Mr. or Mrs. Milquetoast, you'll have arguments that will pop up frequently. We all know key words that we can toss out, and when those words hit it's as if you poked a hornets' nest. But winning or losing those arguments isn't the point. Marriage isn't a contest about who can win or dominate. It's a fluid, ever-moving partnership that is always changing and evolving. That being said, it's obvious that in a working, productive partnership there must be flexibility. That's one of the basic keys needed to survive marriage. The marriages that survive are always a flexible work in progress. The ones that develop a rigid, unforgiving attitude will not necessarily end up in divorce, but perhaps they might as well. (But before you pull the trigger and file those divorce papers, be 100 percent sure your marriage has passed the point of no return. Remember, all marriages, even the best, have problems, and divorce has long-lasting, far-reaching effects on a family.)

I've found out the hard way that there are times when our nerves are on edge and every small, insignificant comment gets a short, snappy answer. Of course, that usually brings the same answer in return, and then it's off to the races.

It happens in every marriage, but the difference in a high-quality marriage is what occurs after the first verbal shots are fired. If there is a realization by both partners that those retorts and are nothing more than a quick, knee-jerk reaction, and they should be quickly dismissed, then it's just a marriage blip that can be quickly put behind them as they move on. However, if eyes flash and the participants dig in for some extended toe-to-toe verbal combat that goes on and on, then there's a problem.

That's the very opposite of going the extra mile or bending and accommodating your spouse. As you can imagine, when you have two emotional partners with no flexibility they will always be arguing about something—right up to the divorce. Some of the biggest screaming, confrontational arguments in marriages have started over the most insignificant matters.

That's when you need to be flexible and compromise. Vertis and I are very much alike—we're emotional, high-strung people and we have a tendency to snap back at the smallest slight. A raised voice or even a change in the tone of our voice can trigger some nasty comments. However, we realized that a number of years ago, and now we take a deep breath instead of snapping back. Well, to be honest, sometimes after a hard day when we're stressed, we don't take that deep breath and for a few minutes we revert to our old ways. No marriage is perfect, and squabbles will occur even in the best.

The key is to shortcut those little fusses and get back on a positive note as soon as possible. Remember this: When there's difficulty in a marriage caused by a disagreement, misunderstanding, or just a plain old dumb remark, stress is on both parties. So it's to your benefit to restore peace—and reduce your blood pressure. After all you're doing yourself a favor. What couple would rather squabble and fight versus cuddling and making love? You sure can't cuddle and make love in the middle of a fuss. (If you don't believe me, try hugging your spouse right in the middle of the next argument you have. I promise, it'll be like hugging a board.)

I know some couples who seem to relish little, petty arguments, and if you examined their marriage closely you'd find it filled with discord. Be careful when you find yourself almost constantly bickering. There's a danger in having too many little scrapes that become cumulative. When you reach a point where you can't be with your spouse for any appreciable time without arguing about sometime, then you know you have a full cup of bitterness, and until something changes, life is going to be miserable for a while. The more you argue with your spouse, the more damage you do to your marriage and quality of life. Occasionally, agreements are just part of marriage, but when they become the defining part of your marriage, you're on rocky ground.

As I just mentioned, sometimes a bad day at the office will trigger temper flare-ups. However, if these confrontations are almost daily and the marriage partners become constantly argumentative (even about the most mundane things) and there is never a resolution of these disagreements, it's time to really analyze your marriage. There's probably some underlying problem that has not been addressed. The key here is to identify the problem and get it out on the table where it can be solved. The longer you ignore something that's disturbing the marriage, the harder it will be to get the relationship back to normal.

I guess a lot of us have been there and struggled back out of the abyss to restart our quality marriage. However, some couples will never return to the pleasurable marriage they once had because of their inflexible attitude. Common logic will tell us that if a marriage once had substance, joy, and pleasure for both, then it is possible to return to that state. In our heart of hearts, a couple may sincerely desire to get back to the good marriage they had before little arguments built up a barrier between them, but the barriers of stubbornness and inflexibility stand in their way. Many salvageable marriages have ended in divorce because of rigid, unbending attitudes.

That's where flexibility and compromise comes in. I've gone back over some rather mean squabbles Vertis and I've had, and when I backed up to the first words of that argument, I was amazed how insignificant those words were. Sometimes, if we were really stressed, just a look would create problems.

Of course, almost 100 percent of those disagreements would have never happened if one of us hadn't been on edge. When things are going great and we're having fun, it's hard to start an argument. That is why a built-in condition of bending and being accommodating is so vital to a marriage. Remember some of the little yelling squabbles you've had and insert bending into that conversation. Most of the time you'd have never taken offense to the comment that started the fuss.

Be like the proverbial water off a duck's back when it comes to reacting to words. That's why bending is better. Going the extra mile is worth it because you can shortcut an argument by not having one. The bottom line is very simple. More quality time in your marriage is available when you're not engaged in a meaningless harangue.

On a purely selfish basis, just think of how many times some stupid argument has spilled over into dinner and spoiled that meal or—even worse—how many times it has spoiled what had shaped up to be a romantic evening until that little screaming hassle came up. More quality time and, yes, more sex, and a lot more pleasant meals are available to couples who bend instead of being inflexible.

It's pretty easy to see what happens to couples who don't give an inch. Sooner or later the stubbornness will build up to the point where that marriage becomes untenable, brittle, and broken. Not giving an inch is not something any marriage needs. It results in constant arguing. Of course, we all agree with that statement, but let's take it apart and apply it to life, or to your real marriage.

It all comes down to respecting the opinion of the other partner, and it's not, "You have every right to your ridiculous opinion." To be quite frank with you, Vertis's savvy in everything from business opportunities to social occasions is sometimes uncanny. She not only contributes to our marriage, she rises to the occasion many times and asserts her position in such a positive, well-thought-out manner that I'd have to be a dolt not to accept her position.

There's a bottom line to bending and accommodating in a marriage. It's very similar to a lot of the precepts that have already been put forth. If we buy the partnership idea as a way to have a quality marriage, and agree it will help us to live the best life possible, then accommodating, bending, and compromising will come naturally. However, some of us—and I include myself—have an argumentative nature. It's harder to compromise in an argument when your genetic background automatically raises your hackles and you have a tendency to snap back. How should a person combat that—what some would call a streak of meanness or, at the least, hardheadedness? And it certainly isn't confined to the male in a marriage.

This is my take: When you're on edge and you instinctively know you're skating on thin ice, then pause before speaking back to your spouse, particularly if it's your nature to throw barbs from the very start of a potential argument. Most of the time just a short pause will tone down your response.

One thing I've noticed over the years: When Vertis and I were young and we were working out the kinks in our marriage, we probably had about the same number of squabbles, but they were longer. Sometimes we wouldn't speak for hours and an insignificant fuss might last a day or two. No more. Now, we may yell at each other, get mad as hell, and cuss like drunken sailors, but it doesn't last. The arguments that lasted for hours when we were young last minutes now. We never let them really bother our quality time together, and missing a meal or intimate moment because of a squabble is unheard of.

The bottom line to the bending and accommodating is very simple. First, develop an understanding where both parties resolve to minimize these arguments. Forget just plain trying not to squabble. It's human nature to yell occasionally, and married couples with any emotional spunk will inevitably have these fusses. So minimize, bend, and put them behind you. If you do, you'll have more high-quality time together, and it'll move you one step closer to living the best life possible.

Premise # 14

Talking is the thread that sews a marriage together

Talk

I've heard numerous individuals comment casually about their spouse, "We never talk." That little phrase may sound innocent to you, and you may be able to identify with the person who said it. But believe it or not, that's an indictment of a sick marriage, and a life that that is less than it should be.

That marriage may not be on the rocks, but it's sure in trouble. We're striving for the best in this book, and one of my key premises is: If you rarely talk to your spouse, you can't possible have a top-quality marriage, and live the best life possible. I don't care how introverted your partner is. It may be hard to believe, but a quality marriage is more talk than anything else. If you reduce the amount of conversation in your marriage, you automatically lower the intimacy, and therefore the quality of your marriage. There is no substitute for talking. I don't care if you have unbelievable sex every day. If you don't have varied conversations throughout the day, you don't have a high-quality marriage or life.

I like to keep it simple, so I'm going to give you an example of how Vertis and I got our relationship off to a great start—by talking. When we were first dating, I took my future wife to a drive-in movie. (That should give you an idea of how long we've been married.) It was only our second date, and at age 21 my testosterone was surging. I had in mind a lot of courting and petting with that good-looking blonde.

However, as we pulled into the parking area and unhooked the speaker from the stand, I started a conversation that I thought would just break the ice, and then we'd do our courting and petting. We were both nervous and timid and were struggling to even have a conversation. Then, for some reason, we relaxed and began to talk about our past and our problems. We realized very quickly that we had something in common—a stressful past. One thing led to another and soon we were sharing our deepest fears and emotions. We shared things with each other that we'd never told anyone. I know that sounds a little far-fetched, and it's certainly not the way an average couple comes to know each other, especially on the second date. However, that long talk opened up our dialogue, and from that moment on there wasn't anything we couldn't tell each other. We still talk about that date. (I actually remember the movie—Raintree County, with Montgomery Clift and Elizabeth Taylor.) Those two hours of conversation brought us closer together than a hundred dates without a deep conversation.

From that moment on, we started becoming emotionally bound to each other. I guess, looking back on our life together, that set the tone for our marriage. We've never had anything we couldn't, or wouldn't, talk about. Talking and sharing our innermost feelings have been a huge factor in our relationship. And it's refreshing to know that I'm an open book to Vertis, and she is to me. You wouldn't believe how many small problems are solved by having an honest, tell-everything marriage. We were so lucky it started on our second date. You know, I really believe I fell in love with Vertis that night.

So my advice is to talk about anything and everything, especially about sex, finances, and work, which are usually the big no-no's, in most marriages. Don't have any subjects that are taboo.

(If that sentence has you shaking your head, then you've got some work to do, and it's heavy lifting—mentally.)

I know the first thing that crosses your mind is that you have some secrets that you haven't told anybody, much less your spouse. What about those? Well, there is an exception to every rule, and maybe those secrets, if they would damage a trusting relationship, should be kept to yourself. I'm sure not going to be the one who encourages you to come clean on everything, to the detriment of your marriage. In fact, I believe in starting with a clean slate when you enter into a marriage relationship. Put the past behind you, unless sharing something will help heal a deep wound from the past.

Let's dig a little deeper in to the "everything" idea of conversation. When I say talk about everything, this is what I mean: Let's look at what is probably the most common conversation a couple can have—an after-work talk. "How was your day?" is usually the lead-in to what can be a short, one-word answer, or a long, animated account by each marriage partner of what happened to them during the time they were apart—who they talked with, what they had for lunch and on and on.

I know it probably crosses your mind that most of the stuff you don't tell your spouse has to do with things you don't think he or she would understand, or would be bored with. But is that true? Is your life so uninteresting that your closest companion would get bored listening to what you did today during an average workday? Yes and no: Yes, he or she would get bored if you tried to describe a technological problem at the office that he or she didn't have a clue about. However, if office politics were involved or personalities flared, you could skim over the technical stuff, and your spouse would probably be interested in hearing about what happened. Consider that everything you say doesn't have to be profound or exciting. Just the sound of your spouse's voice should be enough to hold your interest—and build your marriage's intimacy.

But having an open, transparent marriage is more that hitting the highlights of your day. It's a chance to communicate with your spouse and relive her or his day. I don't care how many text messages you send—and by the way that's not a bad thing—but nothing beats a face-to-face conversation. Many times one or maybe both of the marriage partners have had a stressful day, and relieving that stress by talking should be a primary concern for each of the partners. Listening to a recounting of a rainy day when the carpool didn't work and the basement flooded, or hearing about how a server locked up and deleted half your day's work, might not sound that interesting to you, but when it happens to the one you love, it's important and your partner wants to hear about it. Just re-experiencing what your spouse did on an average day gives a marriage more strength and closeness. It also helps to relieve the average workday stress, which we all live with.

Vertis and I have a time before dinner when we turn on some jazz—sometimes have a glass of wine or maybe a martini—and just talk, talk, talk. And we talk about everything and everybody—nothing is sacred. It's one of the most positive parts of our marriage, and we feel lost when we're traveling and miss that time. My recommendation is to make room for that time just as you would schedule a workout time or any other important business. Talking is the thread that sews a marriage together.

And, yes, I do want to hear about everything that Vertis does and she wants to hear about my day—even the dry holes. Even when Vertis has a pedicure or has her hair done, I'm interested to hear about it. (Hey, some of the stuff she hears at the beauty shop is pretty interesting.)

Communicating with your spouse makes the simple conversations build. Then, when you really do have something important to talk about, your conversation will be much more insightful and intimate than it would be if you just came in out of the cold and said, "I've been transferred to Houston. We need to put the house up for sale." Well, if that husband or wife had talked with his or her spouse day after day about their work, the possibility of being transferred wouldn't have been that much of a shock.

Remember that the "transferred" conversation was not just about one person who announces they're being transferred; it's about the whole family. It should have been just another segment of a partnership conversation. Did the spouse have an inkling they were about to be transferred? Was the spouse brought into the conversation weeks before? If the husband or wife had talked about the details of how the company was opening new offices or making transfers, then the other spouse would slip into the transfer mode a lot easier. Conversations about potential problems or changes in lifestyle should always take precedent when marriage partners discuss the details of their life together.

I know there are some couples who avoid conversations that are too long and detailed. And some individuals might object to what they would call "wasting time talking." Couples with attitudes that limit the time or subjects they will discuss will always have a sub-par marriage. You can't have the intimacy needed for a top-quality marriage if you have that attitude. When it comes to conversation with your spouse, more is always better. But how much is enough?

There is no rule about how much conversation you should have with your spouse. There's only a broad guideline, depending on the amount of time available. However, I believe, at a minimum, you should converse at least two hours every day with your spouse. It can be by phone, text, e-mail, or in person, but remember: Every conversation no matter how insignificant will build emotional ties.

Having a personal conservation comes naturally for some folks, but not for everyone. However, good, deep talks with your spouse are so important that, even if it is difficult for you, make yourself do it, and you will be amazed how much better you understand each other. And if you thought you loved that person before, wait and see how much you love them as you get to know them intimately—by talking to them.

Well, I can hear you now: "But we don't have anything to talk about. When we go out to dinner, we sometimes sit there for 30 minutes and not say a word to each other." Really? Let's take a real-life situation and see if it creates conversation. Let's consider you're sitting at the restaurant table looking at the menu and a cute,—make that a very cute—full-figured cocktail waitress walks up to take your drink order. You order and then go back to reading the menu. Right? Wrong! That's a perfect opening to start an interesting conversation.

The following would be a typical conversation opener from our marriage. Richard, "Hey, did you see that gal's figure!"

Vertis, "Yes, It's amazing what today's medical technology can do."

I think we would all agree those opening lines are a great way to provoke a stimulating conversation. If you're sitting in a restaurant and you and your wife began talking about the physical attraction of a gorgeous woman, wouldn't that stimulate some interesting conversation? Sure it would, but a conversation works both ways if it is to be stimulating to both parties. How about this for a reply?

Richard, "Oh, come on, Mother Nature is just a little more generous to some gals."

Vertis, "Ha! Unless her doctor is named Dr. Nature, she bought those. But I'll agree, someone did a great job."

I know you might be thinking you'd never have the nerve to spit out that opening line to your spouse—no matter what side of the conversation you were on. You may be right, but that's only because you haven't talked about everything in previous conversations.

But let's analyze that conversation. What's the subject? Yes, it's a sexual attraction, which I expressed verbally to Vertis. The reaction by Vertis to a sexual conversation is sure to bring her interest up, and I will guarantee you we'll chatter on and on about something, and the cocktail waitress and our love-life will somehow intertwine. Instead of 20 minutes of dead time, there'll be a stimulating, intimate conversation which started over a full-figured cocktail waitress.

That bit of stimulating chatter is an example of how the best conversations are the ones where you throw out the unexpected to generate interest. How many nights when you were out to dinner have you really enjoyed the evening when the conversation lacked? There is nothing worse than a dead, dull evening where two people struggle to be civil. But really, there's no reason to ever have a dull, pre-dinner talk.

Surely, sitting there with the one you love, you can think of stimulating conversation topics that your spouse will jump into. I think the key to an interesting conversation is for it to be a natural extension of the day's numerous talks, but with something thrown in that will enliven and stir your interest.

If you really want to have a good dinner conversation, then let it be one that is relaxed and a natural part of your day. If you rarely speak to your spouse during a normal day, don't expect a stimulating dinner conversation. Good conversation is like everything else in life: It takes work. Every premise in this book takes a commitment. Some of them may come as a natural extension of your personality, while other will take a real effort on your part. It easy to just coast through a marriage and life without making any commitment on the parts that don't come easy. However, that's the whole point of this book. Marriages that are lived without working on the weak points will never reach their potential, and you will never live the best life that's available to you.

Of course, a good animated conversation is not the whole answer to every marriage problem, but intimate, or just plain, conversation is something that every marriage needs. So, talk, talk, and then talk some more, because you can never tell your spouse too much.

But before we quit this chapter let's go back and revisit the cute, full-figured cocktail waitress. You're already thinking how just letting you eyes wander has caused several upsetting moments—right? Of course, jealousy sticks up its ugly head in every marriage, and if it doesn't—then you've really got problems. But back to the cute cocktail waitress and your wife's comment. First, can you even imagine her making that initial comment? Or let's put the shoe on the other foot: Can you imagine either spouse making that comment without creating a problem? I would be willing to bet the majority of married couples would have some sort of a disagreement when such a comment was made—no matter who made it.

Let's get back to the why that comment is helpful to a marriage instead of destructive. It all goes back to having an open marriage and talking about everything.

Consider this; if your spouse is open and talkative about every aspect of his or her life, don't you think they would understand their partner's sex drive, and how an attractive person of the opposite sex might interest them? Of course, they would. One of the big problems in a marriage relationship is having too much intimate distance between spouses. Let me define what I call the intimate distance—it's not being just physically close. It's the intimacy that evolves over time where you can almost feel the emotions of your spouse and finish their sentences. The greater the distance, the less intimate the relationship. In a truly open marriage, the conversation about the cocktail waitress would be normal and would result in chatty, friendly conversation and certainly wouldn't cause any problems.

Maybe you don't want to be that close to your spouse, and if you don't then this book is not right for you. You really don't want to reach the level of intimacy that a quality marriage has, and consequently you won't ever live the best life that's available to you. However, believe me, if you want the best and most fulfilling life you could possibly have, you'll work to eliminate any and all uncertainty in your marriage, and instead of putting distance between you and your spouse, you'll work to close that intimacy gap.

However, some individuals are so private that their personal life is off-limits to everyone—including their spouse. The problem is, how do you be honest and intimate with someone when they feel you're intruding into the private part of their life? That can be a real problem, especially if it is a part of a life that you've ignored for the last 20 years. Trying to bridge the gap after that length of time is extremely difficult. That's why it's so important to have an early, open dialogue with your spouse.

The open conversation idea of a relationship may seem to be far-fetched because of male and female likes and dislikes. As a male, do I honestly want to hear about how long it took Vertis to buy a pair of shoes? Or does Vertis want to hear about the winning bid I took to build a natural gas pipeline? Yes, I do and yes she does. But, you can't come out of the blue after 15-years of non-communicating and spring buying shoes on your spouse and expect a good conversation. However, if your relationship has been built on a foundation of ever- increasing intimacy and love, then everything your spouse tells you is of interest to you.

Of course, the best way to start a relationship is to build an open, no-secrets communication and work on it over the years of your marriage. Then a story you might tell your wife about going to the woods deer hunting, or one she might tell you about having lunch with an old classmate, will be interesting because you both are so deeply part of each other that what happens to her or him is almost as if it happened to you.

Well, most relationships don't start out that way, so what if your marriage has been built on two separate lives that only come together occasionally and most of the time it's her life and his life? Can this marriage ever find an openness that will improve it and make it more fulfilling to both parties? Yes, it can, but it will take a real focused commitment. Let's take a look at how that might happen. First, we can be realistic and agree that if either spouse, all of a sudden, decided to turn over a new leaf and began to tell the other one everything that happened to them that day, and continue spilling every dark secret and everything about their past, then we can be sure the other spouse would be ready to have them committed. So you can't go from zero to 100 immediately.

First there must be a willingness to actually want this type of relationship in your marriage. Some individuals are naturally private persons and even though they may want the best marriage and life possible, they're not willing to give up their privacy. However, that's not the case with most individuals. Usually, overriding their need for privacy is an even greater need to deepen the relationship with their spouse. It's just that most couples really don't understand how to do that. So let's take an average couple and see how to open up the relationship and build up that foundation of honesty and openness in a marriage.

A good way to think about marriage problems is to understand that if you can't talk honestly about it, you can't solve the problem. First, the couple must have a clear understanding and a commitment to bringing about this deeper relationship in their marriage. A half-hearted approach won't do here. It must be a total commitment. The initial conversations should be shallow, but full of interesting things that happened that day. Don't try to dig deep into the past those first few conversations. The best start to deepening your relationship could be for a spouse to talk about an experience which meant something to him or her, but which the other has been completely oblivious to. Tell it with relish and share the emotion you feel.

Okay, now here's the exception to the open and honest relationship I've been touting. In trying to develop this relationship there will be some rocky and, yes, some boring times. These incidents can shipwreck a relationship quickly because as a couple tries to deepen their relationship they are very venerable. Being venerable is dangerous because emotions are fragile and the wrong word or body language can wreck a relationship, and instead of continuing to open up a marriage, the partner may feel scarred from a thoughtless comment or even a yawn. So tread softly, especially during these first few conversations. And even though they seem totally without merit from your prospective, you must at all costs, act as if these things are interesting and ask questions, lean forward as if you are hanging on every word, and for God's sake, don't interrupt or just sit there silent.

Now, I'll agree that doesn't seem to be an open and honest relationship, but these early conversations are building blocks to get there. As these conversations continue, you'll find the acting part becomes less and less and your emotional level with your partner deepens until the smallest incident in that person's life will be interesting to you. You won't be faking it anymore, and your emotional bond with your partner will strengthen. But don't stop there.

After weeks of opening up with daily problems and thoughts that seem inconsequential, you're ready to go deeper. This may trouble some people, but believe me if both parties in a marriage have a genuine desire to know and be deeply, emotionally attached to the other as a life partner, then there are no subjects that are off-limits.

This is a plan to begin to go deeper. First off, don't hit you partner with some shocking revelation, such as an extramarital affair. He or she might not be emotionally ready for that kind of a shock. However, as your emotional bond strengthens, the depth of your inner thoughts you can reveal to your partner also increases. One day, if you keep bonding emotionally, there won't be a subject that you can't discuss in the utmost detail, and there won't be anything your partner will shy away from or take umbrage.

I know you may be thinking about something deep in your past that would seem so destructive that you wouldn't dare to tell your spouse, but believe me, there will be a time when he or she will empathize with you and when you reveal it to your spouse, it will strengthen your marriage.

But before you go there, let's talk about the road to those deep, off-limit subjects. Let's say you've spent hours talking about the ordinary—the mundane things that involve you and your spouse—and now you can feel a greater intimacy, an openness that you haven't felt before. If you don't feel that way, don't go deeper until you do. Trying to push emotional depth in a marriage is always the wrong thing to do. It can backfire and cause you to actually lose ground in your goal to achieve the highest quality marriage possible.

But let's say you do feel that emotional bond and your spouse has become more and more receptive to bonding with you. Bonding is important because a part of each person shares that bond and when the bond is strongest then the emotional response by each person will affect the other. In other words, what hurts you hurts your partner.

You should start these emotional conversations by going back to your childhood where you might have lingering regrets and fears about things that happened. These experiences may not seem rational or important to your partner, but if the emotional bond you've built up over the past months is truly positive, then your partner will feel as strongly about this experience as you do, and now that person knows you a little better, and emotionally understands you. But this is important: Don't just talk about yourself. Remember that this is a conversation, and conversations are between parties sharing the listening and talking.

So after one or the other opens up about their childhood, there should be a pause—then a question that will automatically give the other partner an urge to talk about his or her childhood. You'll be surprised at how much of our present emotional state comes from childhood experiences. Knowing this about your spouse may give you a much better understanding of why he or she reacts or doesn't react to a situation. Don't just tell the story of weird Uncle Simon at the Fourth of July picnic, but let your partner question different aspects of the encounter, and let you expel—yes expel it from your conscious.

As your partner opens up and relates what may be a long-hidden secret and gets it out of his or her system by sharing it with a caring partner, it can be tremendously therapeutic and can help resolve some emotional problems. The old adage "talk about it" really does work, but only if both are emotionally prepared for it.

A word of caution: Don't dig deeper too quickly. Let a little time pass and let some emotional confessions come from the other party before you reveal your deepest secrets. As this emotional bonding strengthens, you'll find you're becoming "thick as thieves." That right, as you share your bond, you deepen to a new, a more positive, level. That's what we're all striving for, and that's where the next level will take us.

Are you ready for that? The next step in emotional bonding is to share the very core feeling that you've jealously guarded your entire life. It's the "I'd never tell anyone what I did in…" Really? Are there things in your past that are so vile and revolting that even an emotionally bonded spouse would find repulsive? I guess if we're honest we could answer in the affirmative, but before you move away from those dark secrets take an objective look at them, and you'll find time has mellowed them or what seemed to be a horrid situation at age 16 doesn't seem so bad at 35, and it's almost a joke at 65.

Well, for most of us, our deep dark secrets are mostly embarrassing situations we even hate to think about, possibly times when we strayed from the straight and narrow into areas where we now know we should have never gone. Drugs? Sex? Cheating? I don't have to go on and on; you know the special dark places that no one but you has ever ventured. Well, you might ask why on earth you should drag up old affairs or digressions that you had kept hidden for 20 years? That's not an easy answer because there is always a possibility that the bonding and sharing that has brought you emotionally closer is not strong enough to stand a startling revelation. Be sensitive to this, because where you are now after months of emotional bonding, is too precious to risk. However, the risk does have rewards. If your spouse believes you have emptied your most hidden innermost secrets, then he or she will realize the depth of your vulnerability and emotional commitment. Then, and only then can a couple have the intimacy that a complete revealing of their souls can give. It can lead a couple to a plateau that you never thought possible and to an understanding of each other you never imagined could happen.

But, before you take a step that endangers all the effort the two of you have made, be sure where you are emotionally and how your spouse feels. Many times, instead of dropping the complete bombshell of a past digression, bits and pieces can slip out from both parties and lead to the inevitable final opening and sharing of your soul. This is a goal of all marriages—to have a completely open and transparent relationship where each knows everything about the other.

In the final analysis, the best and the simplest way possible to become closer to your spouse is to reveal your innermost—your deepest feelings—and leave yourself vulnerable. Being that exposed might sound like something that would be destructive to you, but to the contrary, only when you're open and accepting—yes and that usually means vulnerable—can you move your relationship to a new, a more personal level. If your relationship is based on a deep love, then your spouse is going to respond to your openness in kind. He or she will open up and the result will be a deepening of your marriage relationship.

But how do you reach that level? It's one thing to talk about completely opening ourselves up to someone else, but yet another to actually have conversations that reveal our innermost thoughts. Of course, unless, as a spouse, we are accepting of the flaws that will certainly come out when we get honest with our spouses. We could endanger the whole marriage concept by using information that was highly personal against the other partner.

Instead of using these personal items to load your gun, so to speak, we should use them to understand the complicated person we married. And yes, believe it or not, we're all married to complicated people. The person you might think is shallow and superficial could be harboring fears that prevent him or her from becoming the person they could be.

When a person reveals their deepest fears or desires, they are available to connect with their spouse and bond that relationship. Only when this happens can a marriage make real strides forward. Real, unvarnished intimacy is the catalyst for positive change in a marriage, and when openness and acceptance occurs, the couple invariably becomes closer. It's one of the basic stepping stones to reaching the ultimate marriage relationship.

So share those secrets, and then marriage confidence will remove jealousy and when that cute, full-figured cocktail waitress comes weaving by, you can share your husband's pleasure and entice him at the same time, knowing his sexual desire is focused for a moment on another woman, but only for a moment. And it works the same way for women. If a man encourages his wife's sexual desire which bursts forth from watching attractive males cavort on stage, and, if he kids and around, he'll reap the benefits—not the Chippendales—from her arousal.

As a final word about conversation: Most of the time we don't intentionally withhold information from our spouses. It's simply that by growing apart we subconsciously don't consider them as worthy of receiving every little tidbit of information we have stored away from our daily life. By forcing yourself to talk and tell the most intimate details of your day to you spouse, you will invariably become closer and more intimate. It's all a matter of talking your way to a top-quality marriage and a great life.

Premise # 15

Your marriage must have a foundation of honesty

Honesty

Should the complete, unvarnished truth be the standard for every marriage, and should every conversation between husband and wife be the exact truth? Will complete honesty help us to live the best life possible? If we answer "no" are we in danger of building a marriage relationship on lies? But what about "yes"? Are there truths, if expressed, that will do absolutely nothing to build up a relationship and would probably damage it? Of course there are, and I would never recommend you tell your spouse something—even though it's the absolute truth—if it damages the marriage relationship.

Everything—including being honest—should be evaluated as to its possible injury or enhancement of a couple's emotional well-being. That's the bottom line, and if it bothers you to dodge the truth or even too tell an out and-out lie, then do your best to get over it. What value has the truth when it's demeaning or hurtful to the one you love? Just remember this: There are no perfect marriage partners, and if our every action and thought were exposed to our spouse, it would be extremely detrimental to the marriage.

That's why the emotional well-being of your spouse must be considered in everything you do in a marriage, and being honest with your spouse is just another delicate building block to help you enjoy a top-quality life. And believe me, honesty is probably the most delicate of the life-building blocks. You will not have the best marriage possible, if you are insensitive to the emotional well-being of your spouse.

Now let's look at some ordinary situations that come up in every marriage. Opportunities to lie or tell the truth come up every day. I'm sure you remember little innocent questions such as, "Does this dress make me look fat?" Or "Does this comb-over look okay?" If you have ever hedged on either of those questions, or other similar ones, then you were lying. And in my opinion, that's okay. Remember the emotional well-being of the marriage must always take precedence over anything—even honesty. I believe there are many times when the plain, unvarnished truth is like a slap in the face. When was the last time you told a new mother her baby was ugly? Or you actually said, "That dress makes you look fat." A truthful statement that is irrelevant to the basic honesty of a marriage must be beneficial, or not said at all. However, don't ever think because you can lie about inconsequential items, you can lie about matters that are critical to the honest, bedrock emotions that underpin a marriage.

But, for a minute, let's get back to the small potatoes: Marriage is full of minor emotional situations that must be handled delicately, and the question about a dress making someone look fat is nothing when compared to some of the hot topics that are everyday occurrences. Let's look at one of those hot topics and see if brutal honesty is the way to proceed.

Your spouse spent all afternoon preparing an elaborate meal for a small dinner party. The guests seemed to enjoy it, but you thought it was next to terrible. Too highly seasoned—cold when it should have been hot—and so forth. The party is over and your spouse is ready for a compliment. What do you do?

No, you don't tell him or her the dinner was terrible! There is no place for that kind of honesty here, because this may seem to be a minor matter to you, but it is not to your spouse. You compliment everything you can imagine about the dinner.

If you were brutally honest you would devastate your spouse. And what would it accomplish? Nothing of course. But if you were kind and considerate and tried to think of how much effort was put into the meal, you would never even think of criticizing it. Believe it or not, a pointed criticism of something that someone in the marriage relationship has invested a lot of time and effort into, is never right. It ignores the emotional well-being of the marriage partner, and when you do that you degrade your quality of life.

Most of us have learned the hard way to be tactful, but we've all been around people who seem to delight in castigating some innocent soul—truthfully, of course. They seem to relish the moment as the truth embarrasses and hurts their target. But what do these people accomplish? They build a reputation for being cold-hearted and ruthless. Not exactly the reputation you would want your spouse to have, and, as you might imagine, you'll never see a person like that live the best life possible.

Well, then is it okay to lie? Yes, sometimes it is, because marriage is an emotional relationship, not only a legal contract. Emotions always are present and when truthfulness is considered, these emotions must be at the forefront of any discussion. To ignore the emotional state of your marriage and spew forth cold, cynical, degrading, albeit truthful statements, is a recipe that will undermine the most solid relationships.

Think of your marriage as an ever-changing, ever-developing emotional organism. Different today than yesterday and different tomorrow than it is today. That's why a marriage is like a newborn baby. It must be handled with the utmost care. And little hateful remarks will disturb your marriage just as a wet diaper will upset a baby.

At the same time, we've all been in situations where the truth was desperately needed, but instead a lie was inserted into the relationship. That's wrong and it cannot be justified on the basis of the other partner's feelings. There is a time when only the truth is right for a situation. Consider an alcoholic husband whose wife won't force him to face his drinking problem, but goes along with, "George, you're just a social drinker and sometimes you drink a little too much." She's lying and she knows it. This is a time for the wife to intervene and at least tell him the cold, hard truth, even if the truth will emotionally upset the marriage partner. If you value your marriage, don't ever tell a lie such as that. A lie of this nature will undermine the marriage where the truth might improve it.

It's an absolute marriage principal that every spouse should be vigilant and truthful if their partner is engaged in anything destructive to themselves. If that's the case they should honestly confront them. Naturally, if it's destructive to your spouse, it will be harmful to the marriage and devastate the couple's quality of life. Nothing but the truth and the whole unvarnished truth is suitable here. And if it is a very serious situation where your spouse is endangering the relationship by engaging in something destructive, you should consider enlisting your closest friends to become part of the intervention.

Remember this: There are no perfect marriages, and all marriage partners have at one time or another strayed from telling the truth, which at face value is normal. But, if a marriage is built upon an underlying foundation of one lie after another, then there is a certainty that someday the truth will come out. And, if those lies are destructive enough and have violated the basic well-being of the couple, the marriage will be in great danger. You can't possible live a good-quality life in such a marriage. The presence of accumulated lies that have been inserted into the relationship will eventually destroy the marriage.

Of course, one immediate thought that comes to mind has to do with the faithfulness of the partners. Since all marriages are built on trust and affection, lies about such things as an illicit relationship will one day come back to haunt the marriage, break down the trust, and reduce the amount of affection present in the relationship. But let's face it; in today's world—if you believe the polls—a large percentage of marriage partners have strayed at sometime during their marriage. According to recent studies, some 35 percent of all marriage partners admit to having affairs. And just consider how many others, while not having an affair per-se, have had serious flirtations with someone other than their marriage partner.

If we consider every misstep to be an unfaithful act, then we have the majority of marriages in this country—the ones that have had an affair or serious flirtation—potentially concealing a lie. Should these marriage partners have a time of confession where every bit of dirty laundry is laid out for the other partner to see? I know just the thought of that would make a lot of marriage partners shudder. So let's be honest and say no. The rationale behind building a marriage that's of the highest quality possible is difficult enough without slinging in some irrelevant stories about old digressions—or maybe even new ones.

However, let's don't just gloss over affairs and their relationship to honesty in a marriage. We all know many marriages that have broken up because of unfaithfulness, and many times someone will say in an offhanded manner, "Oh, so-and-so got a divorce because (fill in the blank) had an affair." Did this simple act of unfaithfulness cause the couple to divorce? Is it the unpardonable marriage sin? No, I don't think so, and I'll tell you why.

But first, we must analyze unfaithfulness and the role honesty plays in the relationship. Of course, we all know the dictionary definition of unfaithfulness, but because each marriage is different from every other marriage, the act of unfaithfulness is also different.

Consider this statement: Should a marriage of 30 or 40 years, one that has all the attributes of a quality marriage, dissolve because one of the marriage partners made a mistake, and that mistake was being unfaithful? To answer that I guess I have to go to my Christian background to give you my take on this one. Yes, I'm familiar with the Ten Commandments, but let's look at the underlying problem that concerns unfaithfulness.

Consider this statement: "All have sinned and fallen short of the glory of God." That's a New Testament quote about sin. Of course, unfaithfulness is a sin, but in my book, and God's book, it's not the unpardonable sin. Just as before God, sin is sin and there are no big sins and little sins. Sin is sin in a marriage, and we should look at lapses in our marriages in that manner. Your spouse's sin—no matter what—is, in your opinion, always worse than your sin. It's human nature. That's why, you can't grade sin! The human factor makes grading sin inaccurate. So, for God's sake—and for your marriage's sake—don't try to do this.

It's the same way in a marriage. An unfaithful act might seem grave if you are the wronged spouse, but is your bitter, unforgiving attitude—that came before the act of unfaithfulness—less or more than the act of unfaithfulness? The seriousness of a particular sin in a marriage always has to do with who committed the transgression. Just as you can't grade sin when it is a sin against God, you can't grade sin when it is against you as a marriage partner.

I contend the sin of unfaithfulness is just another shortcoming, lapse, or sin or whatever you want to call it that occurs within a marriage. A detailed analysis of many marriages that you think broke up because of unfaithfulness would reveal that they didn't dissolve because of that one failing. Usually an affair is only one of a dozen failures within a marriage, and many times, the affair was only a trigger for divorce. Those marriages had failed before the affair.

Since an affair is such an emotional and many times traumatic climax in a marriage relationship, how do you handle it with honesty? Rather than immediately answer that question I would like for us to discuss a marriage with openness where anything can be discussed and debated, versus a marriage where everything the respective marriage partners do is a closely held secret.

Can you imagine what a bombshell an affair would have on a secretive, don't-ask, don't-tell marriage? The shock would very likely unravel the weak marriage. And if we're honest, the separate, private marriage I discussed in a previous chapter, is anything but a quality marriage. An affair that happens in such a marriage many times will be a marriage ender.

But what about an open marriage—one with numerous high attributes? Of course, it would be a blow, but almost certainly not a marriage-ending one. In an open marriage, the person outside the marriage would probably already be known and the flirtation between the spouse and that person would have been noted. The actual act of intercourse might cause some repercussions, but it wouldn't be a total bombshell.

Consider this example of how a couple with a very high-quality marriage might deal with unfaithfulness. Let's say the couple is friends with several other couples. One of the marriage partners of Couple A, and one of the spouses of Couple B began to flirt with each other. First, it's just a foot-rubbing under the table and then more affectionate hugs and then a sneak kiss in the hallway. I know you're nodding, thinking; "Yes, that's just exactly how affairs start." Of course it is, but a majority of the time it's all that ever happens. So how does Couple A, with the high-quality marriage, cope with this flirting? And by the way, the non-flirting partners are probably somewhat aware of what's going on.

Let's consider human nature before we answer that question. The sex drive in adults is one of the strongest urges in our bodies. Flirting happens because it is a natural part of life. It's a strong desire that expresses itself to everyone with an active sex drive, and it's exciting and flattering to everyone concerned. It's extremely hard to resist flirting, and if we knew the exact percentage of married couples that have had a serious flirtation, we might be shocked. Probably close to 90 percent of married couples would admit to serious flirting sometime in their marriage.

So how does Couple A handle flirting? This is my take: They talk about it. Yes, and this is a time for the complete, unvarnished truth. I know if you don't have an open marriage where you talk about everything, that little statement makes you take a deep breath. About the last thing on your mind is to tell your spouse about the hallway kiss when you were with Couple B's wife. But consider this: If you've been married for any length of time, you can tell when your spouse is flirting. They may deny it, but you know them better than anyone. You might not have seen the kiss in the hallway, but you don't have any doubt about the flirting. To lie about flirting sows distrust, and that's the last thing you want in a marriage.

In order to minimize problems that may result from flirting, the person flirting should talk about it. After all, your spouse already knows you've been flirting, so why try to hide it? Tell him or her every detail, and don't try to hide your feelings—if you were excited or flattered. The conversation might go something like this: "Honey, guess who was coming on to me tonight?" (Naturally you're going to lie about who started the flirting, but it doesn't matter.)

"You don't have to tell me. You and—Jill—or Sue—or Cindy—or whoever, were pretty obvious."

"Oh, we were just talking about stuff—you know—kids and football."

"Oh, really? That was it?"

"Well, not quite."

"What else?"

"Oh, a little foot rubbing under the table and when we left, a little more than a goodnight kiss on the cheek."

Now, let's analyze your feelings. If your spouse told you about that level of flirting he or she experienced at a party, would you experience anger, jealousy, excitement, or happiness that your spouse was attractive enough to be flirted with by a member of the opposite sex? Naturally, everyone's emotions are different, especially when considering sexual attractions, but whatever your emotions might be, would you consider this flirtation an act of unfaithfulness? No, of course not.

Let me give you my take on this level of flirting. Don't lie about it! Use it! Let it add rather than take away from your marriage intimacy. It's so much of a natural part of life that to try and squelch it or be upset that it becomes counterproductive. So how do you use it? You may be puzzled by that statement, but consider this: Everyone understands what flirting is, but do we understand our body's reaction to flirting. The sex researchers, Masters and Johnson, demonstrated how the pre-intercourse action of flirting acts as an arousal for men and women. I can guarantee you a flirting spouse will come home from a party with sex on his or her mind—and who is the recipient?

Flirting is just part of life anytime males and females come together, and it's so common that we are foolish to ignore it and act as if it doesn't occur. Wouldn't a marriage be stronger if, instead of lying about it when we are caught flirting, we admitted it and used the arousal within our marriage? Sure it would.

Let's look at flirting in the most realistic manner possible. If we do we'll realize most of the time flirting is just that and even if it's more physical, such as a sneaked kiss, it never goes any further. If that's the case, and it usually is, most adults would be better off to have it out in the open.

Now, let's consider how a couple handles just plain flirting. You know it's happening, and you've talked about it but it's still continuing. In my opinion you shouldn't overreact to this situation. After all do you want to lose a friendship over something that occurs so frequently—to so many couples? I don't want to minimize the danger of constant flirting with the same person, which can lead to an affair, nor do I want to just dismiss flirting as an unnatural part of an adult life.

In order for a couple to handle a flirtation and not have it escalate into an affair has to do with the strength of that couple's marriage. A truly committed couple that has most of the critical marriage parameters going for them has very little risk, even if both partners are flirting on a regular basis. Contrary to what most people think, a top-notch marriage is a lot stronger than you realize, and even serious flirting is not going to endanger it.

Commonsense usually takes over and the flirting partner backs off to maintain that quality marriage. However, on the other hand, a marriage that is fraught with problems, and to be honest, it's really marriage-lite, then flirting takes on a different perspective. Infatuation draws the flirters together and instead of backing off because they fear the loss of a quality relationship, their bad marriage relationship is actually an incentive to consummate the flirting with a full-blown affair. It's this type of an affair that invariably leads to the breakup of the marriage.

And by the way, let me comment about flirtations. I'll be honest, I enjoy a flirtatious conversation with an intelligent, attractive woman much more than I do with a group of men. You won't find me talking football when I can talk to a vivacious woman. But back to flirting.

Actually, what is flirting? All of us can spot an obvious flirt, either male or female, but that's only a small percentage of flirters. Flirting can just be eye contact, or a deep conversation about health care. If the conversation is with someone of the opposite sex, then there is almost certainly some flirting going on. Is that good or bad, or something in-between? I guess you'll have to answer that because it has to do with your intentions. Ask yourself, "What are my intentions when I flirt?" And by the way, whether you know it or not, everyone has some intentions when they flirt.

For most individuals, the intent is nothing more than flirting. If that's the case, the flirting is harmless, and actually enhances the marriage of couples that flirt. That may seem a little strange at first glance, but awareness of your sexuality and the awareness of a person of the opposite sex's sexuality can easily be turned into a positive, private experience by a compatible couple. It's not hard to remember a flirtatious conversation at a dinner party, or some other event that stimulated a later sexual encounter with your partner. Is that bad? No, because that flirtation is being directed back to a couple's sexuality and not to another individual.

But, as we all know, the intent of some flirts is away from the marriage relationship, and sometimes those intentions can destroy a marriage. We must always be aware of this threat even to a strong marriage, and when we are engaged in flirtatious conversation, be sure to stay within the limits of harmless trifling. My rule of thumb is that the flirtation stays at the party and does not continue to any private meetings, phone calls, or text messages.

However, there are times when a strong sexual attraction carries flirting to the act of intercourse, and one of the marriage partners actually becomes unfaithful. How does a couple in a top-quality marriage handle an affair? To understand how a marriage partner in a great marriage could stray, we must realize that sexual attraction has an unbelievable pull on some adults, and even if the person flirting has a top-quality marriage, they can succumb to the desire to have sex. As I mentioned in an earlier chapter, every individual has a different level of sexual desire and while some individuals may easily resist sexual temptation, others are almost powerless to say no. So when an affair happens in a good-quality marriage how does a couple handle it?

This is an entirely different situation than a serious flirting episode, and in order for a marriage to sustain this blow the situation must be handled delicately. I believe if a couple has a relationship that is open, and they have a strong emotional bond, then the affair will be known almost immediately by the marriage partner not involved. When a couple has a good-quality marriage, it is almost impossible to keep something as all-consuming as an affair a secret. They both know. What now?

Well, I must say it again—talk, talk, talk—and for God's sake don't lie about it! Don't accuse, rave, or threaten, just talk to your marriage partner in a frank and candid manner. The offended partner doesn't need to berate the partner that strayed. The very act of straying from the marriage vows and threatening a good-quality marriage is enough guilt. In a situation such as this the solution will come forth, and the solution will almost always be to repair the marriage—not to end it. Honesty will prevail and it will save the marriage.

When a couple with a marriage of worth discusses the benefits of their marriage, they will so strongly outweigh the sensual pleasure gained from the illicit affair that the marriage almost always come out the winner. But it's not enough to just say put it behind us and move on. A complete restoration of the marriage is impossible unless the partner that committed the digression has the resolve to make a serious recommitment to his or her marriage partner, and to end the affair—and stop any flirtation with the person involved in the affair.

However, that marriage is not out of the woods yet. The real danger, after the marriage is repaired, is that the offended party will not forget. The temptation to use the affair as a zinger in an argument is great and the damage it will do—if used on a continuing basis—is massive. So remember this: A good-quality marriage can be revived after an affair, and it can return to the same level as before the affair, but only if complete honesty is inserted in the discussion about the affair, and they both agree never to mention it again.

Before I leave the subject of an affair, I want to reiterate my opinion that an affair is usually not the biggest problem in a marriage relationship. Having an affair is terrible, but it's not an automatic marriage ender. There are many marriage problems that can harm a marriage and to single out one—having an affair—as the worst is wrong. It's wrong because by designating it as the marriage ender, it takes over the life of the people who believe—even if they don't want to end their marriage, they must because one or the other had an affair. If having an affair is the only flaw in a marriage relationship, surely a logical couple can see the worth in all the other positive elements that are there.

So my advice is not to have an affair—of course—but if your marriage finds itself in peril because of an affair, don't feel obligated to end the marriage. See it a lapse in judgment, a sin, or whatever, but don't consider it the unpardonable sin.

But back to lying in a marriage, when it is associated with flirting or an affair. If the act of flirting or unfaithfulness is hidden in a relationship, then inevitably it will sooner or later come to the surface and haunt the couple. When a hidden affair is exposed it can cause serious damage to a marriage relationship. So my recommendation is to talk about the initial flirting as soon as it happens and then don't conceal anything as it proceeds. When it comes to telling the unvarnished truth in a relationship, as it relates to flirtations and affairs, don't hold back. Tell your spouse exactly what happened. Honesty must be complete and current.

However, if we agree that flirtations and affairs have a special place in a couple's truthfulness, what about other subjects? In my opinion, it's really a matter of weighing out the pluses and minuses of your marriage. Again, let me repeat myself: If an out-and-out lie is better than the emotional peril it would put the marriage in, then by all means—lie. This is my solution. And it's not a cut-and-dried one because each marriage is a different, complex organism. Marriages are delicate, and as you see your marriage evolve you may come to the point where you can just toss off flirting as trivial. But don't consider that to be the case in every mature marriage. Some adults have an extremely sensitive nature, and flirting might be devastating to that marriage. What might work for one marriage could easily disrupt or destroy another. Sensitivity in a marriage is critical.

I think we all understand the basic principal of marriage honesty, and as we live out our marriage we try to operate somewhere in between an out-and-out lie and the cold, hard truth. I think you can see that sometimes the cold, hard truth cuts and hurts. It's not that you aren't being honest, it's that you are being a lot more honest than you need to be. Honesty comes in a big overall package and in a quality marriage the truth is repentant with bumps and ridges, and believe it or not, those bumps and ridges are lies.

If we agree that honesty is not an absolute, then how do we balance honesty in a marriage and yet keep that foundation strong and intact. We sure don't want to build a marriage on lies. Do we? Let's look at building a marriage on lies. Sometimes a marriage becomes lie orientated and one lie builds on another until the whole marriage becomes so top-heavy with lies that it collapses.

Let's use sex as an example. Yes, we all know that sometimes sex can be so good that you get up from bed and just marvel at what just happened. Other times, because of stress or physical problems, it becomes a struggle, and you are frustrated and depressed. This is where honesty comes into play.

If every time you had sex you lied and said it was the best ever, even if it was terrible, you'd be digging a deep hole in your marriage; a hole that would someday collapse around you. And if it didn't destroy your marriage, it would create a deep measure of distrust from your marriage partner. So, how do you walk that fine line and keep honesty to the forefront and yet don't bruise the feeling of your spouse? Believe me, it's not easy, but if we flash back to that intimate dialogue that couples need, then we can see how a delicate conversation about the most intimate part of a marriage can be discussed while both of the marriage partners remain calm, loving and concerned. Yes, concerned, because a marriage partner should be concerned about his or her partner in every aspect of their life.

When we consider honesty in a marriage I believe it should be intertwined with an intimate sharing of each other's lives. If that level of sharing permeates a marriage, then the question of honesty is almost irrelevant. You don't deliberately lie to your closest companion, but neither do you deliberately say things that hurt them.

Remember, having an open, honest dialogue in a marriage is difficult, but it is a critical step in creating a strong emotional relationship. Many couples have a less satisfying relationship than they could have because they don't reach this level of emotional commitment. However, if a couple does have an open, honest relationship and they treat their marriage delicately in all of their actions and conversations, the basic underlying honesty in that marriage will move that couple toward the high-quality marriage we all desire, and they will have taken a giant step closer to living the best life possible.

Premise # 16

You can't have the best marriage and live the best life possible with a negative attitude

Live a Positive Life

This premise is so simple I hesitated to put it in the book. However, as I reflected on how many couples seem to live in negative misery of their own making, I decided to include it. It's not as simple as living without a negative attitude, it's more like living with a positive attitude. Think of the old adage, "Is the glass is half empty or half full?" Are you viewing life as "half empty?"

But it's more than a simple attitude: First it's a matter of recognizing that one or both of the marriage partners are exhibiting a negative outlook on not only their marriage, but life in general. Sometimes that outlook is buried deep in their subconscious. Until that person, or maybe both of the marriage partners, recognizes that a negative attitude is pervading their marriage, they are always going to be living a sub-par life. They can't possible live the best life possible with a negative attitude about life.

Of course, a positive mental mindset is something physiologists have touted for years. While we nod our heads in agreement we sometimes—maybe inadvertently—are living the direct opposite, and it's not just a matter of treating your marriage with a positive attitude. It's having a positive attitude about every aspect of life, from sports to politics. However, let's be honest: Attitude is much more important in a marriage relationship. That's because the emotional bond between marriage partners is so close—or should be. If a marriage partner has a negative attitude then it is bound to rub off on the other partner, resulting in a degrading of the marriage relationship. I can think of several couples I can't stand to be around because of their negative view of life. No restaurant is ever good enough, and they haven't seen a worthwhile movie in years. It even shows on their faces as, over the years, frowns deepen those wrinkles.

Sometimes a marriage fails or at least founders and certainly never reaches its potential just because of the negative attitude of the couple. That marriage may not have any more flaws than the average marriage, but for some reason there is a spirit of bitterness and recrimination that seem to pervade the marriage, and many times it is present in both parties. I'm sure a physiologist could spend hours delving into the intricacies and problems of couples with negative attitudes, and still not pin down exactly what was causing the problems.

In my experience, sometimes the cause is simple—he married a bitch, or she's married to a real jerk. Well, if you really are married to someone that really fits those categories, I'd be the first one to say, "Find a good lawyer and get a divorce." Life is too short to be miserable because of a bad choice in mates. Not every marriage is worth saving.

However, most of the time, you married a rather delightful person who swept you off your feet. But now things have cooled off and after years of pretending everything was all right—as you watched your marriage go downhill—you've reached the point where you're thinking about divorce. Your attitude and your spouse's attitude have degenerated into a dark, moody tolerance. You can barely stand to be around him or her, and everything he or she does is an irritant. You're having real trouble understanding why you married that person.

But let's try to be honest about your evaluation of this wounded marriage. If you do, you'll probably realize that he or she didn't change overnight, and you're not only the aggrieved one, you're some part of the problem. It's a rare marriage when only one of the parties is completely to blame. So let's take the case where the marriage problems are equally divided. It's 50 percent your fault and 50 percent your spouse's fault. Now, I know there's not one person reading this book who will agree that 50 percent of their marriage problems are their fault. It's human nature to believe your spouse is mostly to blame. But humor me for a minute and let's see what, if anything, you can do to salvage your marriage, and even if you aren't in dire circumstances, how you can move your marriage up another notch toward our goal of a quality marriage where you can live the best life possible.

In order to do this you must readjust your thinking. Instead of grinding your teeth at your spouse's flaws, I want you to put them out of your mind—at least temporarily. Your thought process must change and you must be willing—for a while, to ignore every negative thing about your spouse. At this point it might help to think back to when you were dating and the early years of your marriage. In every marriage there was a positive beginning, and there were things about your spouse that you adored.

Now here's the hard part. I want you to make a list of all of your spouse's best qualities. Start with why you fell in love with him or her, and consider every possible positive quality this person has. Elaborate every way you can imagine until the list reads like Mr. or Mrs. Wonderful. It may take some time to do this, so put an incomplete list aside for a few days, and, as little things cross your mind, jot them down. If there's a lot of bitterness in your marriage, it may be hard to be objective, but it's critical to do so, or you'll never be able to have a better quality marriage.

After you finish your list, sit down with your spouse and talk with him or her about improving your marriage relationship. Don't expand the concept at this point. Marriage is a partnership and unless your partner cooperates, you've really got an uphill battle. However, unless your spouse is through with the marriage, he or she will probably be willing to give this a try. When you do get cooperation, slowly go over your list with your spouse. If you've had a lot of negative vibes in your marriage, your spouse is going to be shocked when you start reading a list of his or her assets and positive qualities.

However, human nature is such that when you began to espouse the positive qualities of your marriage partner, they'll be more receptive to the concept. Then after you have buttered him or her up—so to speak—ask your spouse to take some time and make a list of your best qualities.

Give it some time, but after a couple of days both of you should have your lists. Now comes the hard part. Explain to your spouse that, starting right now, you're only going to praise and not criticize, smile instead of frown, touch, hug and show warmth, and you expect him or her to do the same. The criticism you once had is now praise and instead of frowning, you're going to smile, touch and show warmth. From that moment the marriage partners are going to accentuate the positive and downplay the negative, and show love and affection whenever possible.

Let me warn you, it will be especially hard for the first few days, because you're breaking a bad habit, and it's just like quitting smoking. You'll have to bite your tongue, as you ignore his or her obvious flaws, but instead bringing up those faults, you'll touch, and praise your spouse. If you can get through the first week or so, I think you'll be amazed at the changes in your spouse.

Maybe you bought this book because you wanted to make your husband or wife change. If you did that's perfectly normal. And, if before you started this program you tried to nag him or her into changing, that's also normal. However, this concept of accentuating the positive works in reverse. To get the changes you want, you must approach your spouse in a positive manner. Believe it or not, after a few weeks he or she will began to change, not because you nagged him or her, but because your spouse feels such a positive affirmation of your love and affection. As the dark mood of your marriages changes, they'll be much more eager to change and please you.

Love, kindness, and consideration will accomplish more than frowning and nagging. The final result—and it may take months—will be to change your marriage relationship into a more caring and loving one and take another step toward the elite high-quality marriage you seek, and it will be because your marriage is now underpinned by a positive attitude. One more step toward living the best life possible.

Premise # 17

In order to have a top-quality marriage, you must touch, hug, pat and embrace—you must be a serial toucher

Touch

What a simple-sounding chapter. I know it does sound trite to include something as ordinary as touching in a marriage-life manual. Well, I decided to add it to the book because I believe having successive physical contact with your marriage partner is vital to a successful marriage, and if you want to live the best life possible, you'll be a serial toucher.

Of course, all marriage partners touch, but there's touching and then there's what I call "serial touching." You may be a handholding, hugging, kissing couple, and if you are, you'll blow right through this chapter. I hope you are, but as I watch friends and even total strangers of the opposite sex interact, it's obvious there are more non-touchers out there than serial touchers. The goals in this chapter—if implemented—will make a remarkable change in a non-toucher's marriage.

I'm convinced the physical act of touching is one of the most overlooked positive facets, when marriage relations are analyzed. After all, the whole idea of having the best marriage possible is to enhance all of the positive emotions between two individuals. There are a number of keys to a successful marriage, and they're all interconnected emotional reactions. In my opinion, touching is one of the most overlooked of the critical emotional items in a marriage. There are many marriages where physically touching the marriage partner is infrequent, and I can guarantee those are not top-quality marriages. Why is touching so important? Let's consider some of the reasons in this chapter.

Touching can be as simple as your spouse's hand on your arm, which can turn your frown into a smile. It's so ordinary, yet so underrated. In this chapter I want to explain why and how touching can make a difference, and that difference can be huge in some marriages. Touching is another very important building block that can move a marriage up another notch. Wouldn't you love to discover something so simple that could improve your marriage and increase the emotional bond?

However, as we'll see, there are several types of touching, and not all touching means the same thing. Let's look at the basics. In order to touch we must move to within an arm's length of the individual we intend to touch. Whether you realize it or not, just moving into that private space triggers a reaction from that person—and a reaction from you. Sometimes that reaction is positive; other times it's negative.

Every psychiatrist can tell you that all individuals have this private space. It is the space inside an arm's length distance. If that distance is penetrated by someone intent on harming you, then your reaction will be one of defense. That distance in our minds represents the distance between us and immediate danger. Was this response ingrained in humans from the beginning of history, for our protection? Maybe, because when that space is entered by someone it does trigger a response.

If you feel threatened, your response is anger or fear and your adrenalin pumps; but if you feel the other person's love, warmth, or friendship, then the response is just the opposite. Let me give you an example of how I felt recently when someone came into my space and grabbed me around one of my legs. No, I wasn't fighting off a burglar, it was my 5-year-old granddaughter, whom

I hadn't seen in a few days. She was glad to see me, and she ran up and hugged my leg. A warm, positive feeling swept over me. What if she had just stopped a few feet away and smiled or maybe waved? Would I have felt the same? No, or course not.

But what about adults reacting to other adults entering their space? Remember the bully at school, when we were young, who got in our face and threatened us. Our adrenalin pumped, fists doubled up and our heart pounded. It was a violation of our space, which we knew was a threat, and our body reacted.

But let's focus on the positive reactions we have when someone comes into our space. All of us can remember a time when we were talking with someone of the opposite sex, and that person moved closer and closer until they were well within our space. What did you feel? Well, let me tell you my recent experience where someone entered my space. We all have hundreds of these experiences, but I remember this one very well. It was a couple of months back when Vertis and I were attending a dinner party of about 15 couples. I knew everyone in the room, and I was having a great time sipping an excellent Burgundy and talking with good friends. I was chatting with several people who had all inadvertently positioned themselves just outside of everyone else's space. It's the natural conversation distance, and unless the room is so crowded that you are forced to stand closer, most people will stand and talk just outside of yours, and their private space.

I talked with this group of friends for a few minutes, and then I drifted out of the conversation, walked over and leaned against a fireplace mantel. I wasn't trying to be antisocial, I was just looking across the room deciding on which group of friends I would join. It was a great party, and, since the party was well into the cocktail hour, the wine had picked up the level of conversation. But suddenly things changed. An extremely flirtatious and very attractive woman, one I knew fairly well, walked by, smiled, and then deliberately turned back and stopped to talk with me. I might add that I consider her the most feminine, and—outside of Vertis—the sexiest woman I know. We had a little welcome hug and a polite kiss on the cheek (after all we're Southerners), and, after a few minutes, she moved in closer—inside my space. Then she whispered a bit of juicy, harmless gossip in my ear. The talk and smiles became friendlier, and soon she was well inside my space, and I could feel something happening to me. Of course, the reaction we all have in situations such as this is subtle and probably not noticed by the other participant in the conversation.

What was my reaction? It was probably exactly what yours would have been. I smiled more and laughed at little jokes and my blood pressure and heart rate went up a few points and a few beats. That was stage one. Then the conversation and the closeness moved to a new level. She put her hand on my bare arm. Wow, it was a touch—an innocent touch—which moved my awareness of her and the conversation to a new level. Now, I was enthralled as this sexy woman yanked my emotions around until I was like a dog on a leash. Another close whisper of gossip and her cheek brushed mine. Now I moved to a perpetual smile, squeezed her arm as we talked and was thoroughly enjoying myself. Well, cold water was suddenly dashed on this flirtation when the host called, "Dinner is served."

I reflected back on that night a few days later, and as I thought about my reaction, which, by the way, was just a flirtation that I laughed about with Vertis later, I decided to see if I could achieve the same reaction from another person in my social group.

I had the opportunity a week later, at another party. Was my previous reaction confined to the foxy friend, or was it indicative of a normal response to an attractive member of the opposite sex? I know that's not the proper way to approach friends at a cocktail party, but since my little experiment was certainly harmless, I wanted to see if my response could be replicated with another person. I waited until the cocktail hour was well under way, and the talking became animated. Then I walked over to a divorced friend, very attractive, but unattached and standing alone, and I started a conversation with her. As we talked I deliberately moved closer, complimented her shoes, and then I put my hand on her bare shoulder. Yes, that touch moved the experience into another level for both of us. It was exactly the same response that I'd experienced from my earlier encounter. It was the power of touching. After a few minutes, we were both excited, smiled and were animated enough that Vertis asked me about the conversation later.

After we were home and lounging in bed, we started talking about my flirting. And, by the way, she wasn't exactly innocent herself, and our sexuality toward each other increased to the point where we began to cuddle, touch, and kiss. We made love after a few minutes and it was extremely positive. Did our flirtations with other people entice us to have sex? Well, let's just say that it was a part of the heightened sexuality that many couples experience after being flirted with.

However, I didn't have any thoughts about the attractive divorcee whom I'd flirted with as I made love to Vertis. It wasn't the person I flirted with; it was the experience of touching that moved my level of sexual interest higher. It was the same way with Vertis.

Yes, that was flirtation, and sexual flirtation does cause that reaction, but flirtation with your eyes, and in conversations are only small parts of the sexual attraction that is inherent in flirting. Touching is the primary instigator of sexual attraction. But I know you're thinking, "Why are we talking about touching other men or women when we're trying to strengthen our marriage?"

Well, it's simple: Unless we understand the importance of touching, and how critical it is in a marriage relationship, we'll be missing out on one of the more positive techniques to enhance a marriage. I can't over-emphasize the importance touching to a marriage, and I don't mean just the touching that happens before sexual intercourse. No, it's touching when you get out of bed in the morning. Touching when you leave for work. When you return from work, or when you walk through the park—holding hands.

You may have worked for months and months to talk and share your days and even your deepest emotions, but if you have only confined your touching to a sexual encounter, then you are never going to deepen that emotional relationship you've been working so hard to achieve. Multiple touching is so important that it can't be overstated. Touching by itself moves a marriage relationship to a new level, and it can, with just a touch, remove a barrier that is there from some disagreement. If you don't believe me, the next time you and your spouse have a disagreement try touching. You'll find it very hard to stay angry with someone who's touching you.

I'll have to admit there are some people who don't know how to touch. Touching and violating someone's space is foreign to them, and they can't make themselves do it. They aren't asexual, just shy. What do I tell someone who has an aversion to touching or being touched? This is what I tell them. It's like the first time you played tennis. Your strokes were all wrong and every time the ball came your way you panicked and usually hit a terrible shot. However, as any tennis coach will tell you, just keep hitting balls and your game will improve. So just as your tennis game will improve with practice, your touching game will also. But your tennis game won't improve nor will your touching improve unless you become a regular player.

If you are a non-toucher, you can't change overnight, so don't try to. If you've been a non-toucher for most of your adult life, for God's sake don't run into the room and start randomly touching your partner or anybody else for that matter. Your partner and friends have in their minds your M. O. and if you change anything about your personality that quickly, it will cause the people who know you best to suspect you've had too much to drink or worse. Let me give you another real- life example of how a change in your actions, related to touching, will be noticed.

We're good friends with a couple and the husband is a true non-toucher. However, recently, as he left us with a group of friends, he actually hugged Vertis and kissed her on the cheek. When he left the room the two other couples in the room, as well as Vertis and I, just shook our heads and everybody said at once, "Did you see that? I've never seen _______kiss anyone on the cheek!" So be careful you non-toucher because your friends have you pegged and they will notice any change in you actions, if they are abrupt. Here's how you should move up from a non-touching to a toucher.

You should start with small almost inconsequential touching—patting, squeezing hands, or shoulder hugs. Don't think you can mimic one of your friends who is a real serial toucher. I know a woman—very cute I might add—who not only hugs but kisses—on the lips, all her men friends. It's just her way, and she has been doing it for years. She is a true serial toucher. Her friends expect it and no one thinks anything about it—well, except the guys she kisses. But you can imagine how that reception would be received if a serial non-toucher came into the room and greeted friends that way?

For someone who is uncomfortable with touching, the most important thing to remember is that touching must be casual and natural, and continue from one party or event to the next. Don't touch, hug, and pat for a day or two and then not lay a hand on your spouse for another week, or they'll take that to mean you're withdrawing affection, and your emotional bonding will start to come unglued. Your goal is to make touching a natural extension of your positive love emotion, and if it is, then the very act of touching will build on those positive elements that you have tried to create, and the affections two people have for each other will naturally increase.

Of course, touching can take all forms, but some touching creates a more positive feeling than others. As I mentioned in the earlier chapter on sex, many Americans have abandoned the marriage bed for twin beds or sometimes separate bedrooms, or they have giant king-size beds that are so large they may as well be in different counties. Because the marriage bed is such a wonderful opportunity to increase intimacy by touching I want to quickly mention it again. If you're one of those sleep-apart couples, then you're missing one of the best opportunities to increase intimacy with your partner.

Sleeping close together—cuddling—is one of the primary subliminal impulses of all humankind. It started early in human history from the caves of Africa and continues to the condos of Manhattan—and for a good reason. The very act of cuddling creates a closeness necessary for the preservation of the species—a bonding. It's protection of the female by the stronger male, which results in emotional strengthening and subsequent bonding that will give the couple a better and more satisfying relationship. So toss out those twin beds and king-size beds, get a queen-sized bed, and start cuddling again like you did when you were first married.

Sometimes we let our little sleeping quirks stand between building a stronger relationship. Don't let that happen. As Americans, we've reached the state where I and my and the most important things in our lives, and anything that inconveniences us is automatically thrown out. But we're making a big mistake when we sacrifice a small amount of getting used to for a better long-term relationship with our spouse.

So touching is important, if you want to build on the base that you've worked on for these many months. Let's review that for just a minute. Touching connects us like nothing else can. An affectionate touch, hug, rub, or a full frontal squeeze is not only a smile-provoking response, but it's a deeper response that we don't see. It turns on an emotional trigger deep within us that was implanted sometime during the early years of mankind's development. When that response is triggered, then the emotional gain although small, is cumulative and positive.

Just think of every touch or hug as a building block that will make your marriage more positive and fulfilling. Moving up from a brush on the cheek each morning to a full frontal hug, squeeze and kiss can put a spark of life into a listless marriage. Touching isn't the wonder cure for an ailing marriage, but it certainly is a big step in the right direction.

We can summarize touching as the physical act where your hand, arm, or other parts of your body come in contact with another individual. Deep within our genetic background, affectionate touching is linked to a wide range of emotions. If you're trying to enhance the positive emotions in your marriage, then to touching is one of the easy ways to increase the intimacy in your marriage.

You might think of the benefits in reverse. Let's say you only made physical contact with your spouse when you had sex. (I'm sure that's an extreme case, but not that extreme if you question many married couples.) A couple that doesn't touch on a regular basis will not have as affectionate a sexual experience as one that touches. Touching is probably the most natural emotion enhancer that we have within our system. If we don't touch, we are wasting a part of our emotional well-being.

Touching should be the most natural thing a couple can do. That doesn't mean a greeting with a hug or a kiss on the cheek will suffice. No, touching is so much more than that. It should start as soon as you are together in the morning with little things as simple as an affectionate pat, or hug. It should continue throughout the day with a hundred little things as small as brushing against each other.

Then at night, the intimacy that has been building throughout the day should culminate with a closeness, a cuddling which may or may not lead to a sexual experience. If it does lead to sex it will be a natural extension of the emotional intimacy that has been building all day. However, every night doesn't end with sex, and if both partners aren't in the mood for sex, then the closeness of sleeping together and touching will carry on until the time is right.

A closing thought: You can't have the ultimate, quality marriage and you'll never live the best life possible unless you and your spouse are serial touchers.

Premise # 18

You must be your spouse's best friend

Your Best Friend

I guess, if you're in a marriage with problems, the little phrase, "Be your spouse's best friend and thrive on togetherness," could make a shiver go up your spine. If it does, then you don't have the good-quality marriage you could have. But if you realize your marriage has problems, and you'd like to see that relationship improve, then this chapter is right down your alley.

Actually, having your spouse as your best friend will be the natural result of working toward the goals in the previous chapters. If you follow the recommendations set out in the 18 previous chapters, then you won't have to work at being your spouse's best friend—you will automatically reach that plateau.

You may be in one of the millions of marriages where a couple's lives are so detached that they rarely see each other, much less consider the other to be their best friend. And you might say, "My marriage isn't that terrible." And, you might point out, that too much togetherness might cause you to get on each other's nerves. And absence makes the heart grow fonder. And on and on, as we rationalize.

That is pure rationalization, and every bit of it is false. But let's get to the crux of the matter: Why make a big point out of being your spouse's best friend?

Well, to get right to the point. I believe most marriage problems that cause marriages to fail, or never reach their potential, are because the partners haven't reached the best-friend level of marriage. Those marriages may look successful to an outsider, but deep within their relationship there are problems. And when a marriage has problems, you can never be a best friend with your spouse—and you can sure forget living the best life possible.

Those problems are keeping untold numbers of marriages from ever reaching their potential, and the bottom line is: Unless a couple jointly commits to solving their marriage problems, and becomes best friends, they'll never have the marriage, or life, they could have. Obviously, the problems in their marriages has relegated those couples down several notches from a quality marriage-life plateau.

Let's consider the first point about "too much togetherness." It's not the "being together" that causes tension; it's an underlying difference in viewpoints, desires, and goals of the marriage participants. Obviously, if you're not together, then these differences won't come to the surface as often. However, these differences are still part of a marriage, and unless they are addressed, they'll continue to keep those marriages from being all they could be. But, surely you would agree that staying apart to keep from facing marriage problems is not the ideal marriage situation.

The premise of togetherness is not a forced putting up with your spouse, it's the very opposite. It's wanting to be with your best friend because it's the most enjoyable part of your day. The whole point of surviving marriage and reaching that elite status most of us are striving for is to thrive on togetherness. To bask in togetherness. To exult in togetherness. Togetherness is the key to having the best marriage possible, and only when you do that, will you live the best life available to you.

But before we start delving into being your spouse's best friend, let's clear the air on one point. I'm not saying you should live your life locked at the hip, doing everything and being together all the time. The question is: What is the optimum relationship time a couple should try to achieve? If we eliminate our work and sleeping time, we still have around eight hours available. That amount of time will easily allow you four hours with your spouse, and that should be a goal for your marriage. If you have other activities that prevent you from allotting that much time with your spouse, then you should reduce the time spent on them, until you achieve at least an average of four hours a day with your partner.

I've spent most of this book giving guidelines that, if followed, would strengthen and improve your marriage and life. I think everyone has a goal to attain the best marriage level possible and in doing so be able to live the best life possible, but if we ignore the basic guidelines, especially the one about becoming our spouse's best friend, we'll never reach that elite plateau we're striving for. If you work on all the other guidelines in this book being your spouse's best friend will be the natural outcome. It really can't work any other way.

This may seem a little fuzzy, so why not delve into becoming your spouse's best friend? Volumes have been written on marriage compatibility, and we still don't have all the answers. However, we do have some of the answers, and it comes down to the very nature of friendship. First, think about your friends—go all the way back to your childhood—and think about your best friends. Then, for just a few minutes, think about what you did with your friends. What you played. The movies you saw together. List everything you can possibly think of that you did with your friends.

When you make that list, you have the basis for making your spouse your best friend. If you and your spouse are working together, and you have a list of pleasurable actives that you both enjoy, then you have the basis for friendship.

But let's just say when you compare your list with your spouse's list, it seems as if his or her likes and dislikes are so divergent that to enjoy being together and doing the same things is impossible—and it is, unless the marriage partners try to bridge that gap or add relationship items that both can enjoy. Of course, there is always a time for spouses to diverge and go their separate ways, and enjoy a break in their routine. But remember that you can take that too far, because if done to excess, it will lead to separate lives where you only sleep together.

To be married to someone and have sex as the only thing you have in common is like watching a football team warm up and then not watching the game. Yes, sex, as I have mentioned earlier, is sometimes the glue that holds a marriage together, especially during those early years when all the rough edges of two individuals are rubbing together. But if you're hanging on to your marriage relationship with sex as the only thing you have in common, then, sooner or later, your marriage will disintegrate. The less you have in common the greater the chances your marriage won't make it, and the more separate your lives will become.

Let's go back to you and your spouse's friendship lists. Within those lists you'll find the basic framework to make your spouse your best friend. Some of the items will jump out at you. For example, maybe both of you follow the same sports team or enjoy a good dining experience. Step one is to identify those easy items that both of you enjoy. Of course, you don't need to be told that these easy, common items are the stepping stones to build your relationship. By emphasizing those items you'll automatically become closer just by having a good time together. That's the very nature of friendship. Enjoying each other, by doing things that are enjoyable to both.

Well, step one is easy. But as you look at your lists there will be things that are so divergent that you can't imagine doing them with your spouse. How do you resolve these issues? It's not easy, but it can be done. First, identify the individual items and put them into two categories: Non-threatening and threatening. I know those categories sound a little grim, but let me explain. The non-threatening category contains things that one partner does that the other marriage partner just doesn't have an interest in doing. It may be as simple as collecting stamps. Certainly there's nothing wrong with collecting stamp—is there? Well, there's stamp collecting and then there is, "Stamp Collecting!"

Spending a few hours a week keeping up a stamp collection isn't a problem, but spending four hours a day (and lots of money) is. Therefore, when you decide if something is non-threatening in a marriage relationship, time must be inserted as a factor. To be on the non-threatening list an item must be truly a neutral with your spouse. I think it's a positive part of a marriage to have hobbies and relaxing activities that take up incidental amounts of each partner's time. It's actually healthy.

But now back to the list: If your list is breathtakingly lengthy and requires hours and hours of being separated from your partner, trim it. Keep it balanced with the other partner's list. No more than 25 percent of your free time should be spent away from your spouse on these items.

The non-threatening list is the easy list to make, and it shouldn't be difficult to work out a reasonable amount of time for each partner to "do their own thing." However, the threatening list is tougher. For something to go on the threatening list, it must be an activity that the other spouse believes is a threat to the marriage. The word threat may be too harsh, but the principal is such that when one marriage partner believes an activity or habit is distasteful, or obsessive, or maybe even inappropriate, the marriage has a problem and, believe me, little problems can eventually bring down a marriage.

It may be that the other partner really believes this item shouldn't be on threatening list, but on the non-threatening list. Well, it's not that partner's job to make his or her threatening list. The threatening list must be made by the other partner. That list is made from the perspective of the other spouse, as he or she examines all issues they believe pose a threat to the marriage. Obviously, your threat list will probably be aimed at your partner's flaws—flaws in your opinion.

Which brings us to the tough part of ironing out marriage differences. Sometimes, in order to build a relationship you must give up something. I call this, "Removing the thorns from your marriage."

If the thorns aren't removed, they'll act as a continuing irritation and as your marriage matures, they can be the deciding factor in surviving marriage. However, I do want to make myself clear on one important part of the marriage thorns subject: Usually, there are just as many thorns on one side as the other. Those thorns, which one partner may want to put on the non-threatening list, can't be dismissed if the other partner disagrees. There's no difference in a continuing irritation, which may seem to the partner that is the perpetrator, insignificant, that a blatant, disgusting habit in the opinion of the other. They are both thorns and to the offending party they are equally important.

But let's digress to an earlier chapter, "A Marriage Partnership". Within the marriage there is no situation more important that having a partnership when dealing with the thorns in a marriage. If you really want to send your marriage down the river of no return, insist your partner remove all his or her thorns from the marriage, and in spite of what your spouse may say, refuse to remove yours. Many times removing thorns can be a barter situation. "I will, if you will." You fill in the blanks in your marriage and see if that doesn't help to solve some of your marriage problems.

Well, if improving a marriage was only as easy as solving step one and step two. However, in many, or I might say most marriages, these two steps make up only 20-to-30 percent of the interactions between couples. The heart of the marriage is the other 70 to 80 percent of day-to-day living. How do two people with different backgrounds, likes, and dislikes reconcile their differences and build to the best friend basis? I think many times the little likes and dislikes are harder to overcome than a biggie like—say—quitting smoking.

Consider a couple who dated for a year or so and now are married and trying to make their marriage work. They really do have a job cut out for them. Consider that 50 percent of all marriages in this country fail and you can understand how tough the job is. In my opinion, the primary cause of marriage failure is incompatibility. I know that's kind of a cop-out, but if we consider the underlying causes, I think we'll agree. Couples who can't, or won't, seek compatibility usually end up getting divorced or hanging in there and making life miserable for each other. Let's examine how compatibility works.

The bottom line in compatibility is something I've mentioned before: being your spouse's best friend. That's it! As marriage partners blend their desires and pull the thorns from their marriage, they automatically become closer and closer. They want to be together because they enjoy each other and they take pleasure in doing enjoyable things in the company of someone who enjoys the same things. Does that sound simple? Well, it is. But sometimes the simplest of solutions are overlooked. Well, I guess I haven't really answered the why you would want to be your spouse's best friend, have I? No, not directly, but indirectly.

The whole premise to this book is that the best possible way to enjoy life is to be married, and not only married, but to be married to your best friend. If you reach the level of surviving marriage where you are your spouse's best friend, then you have made the moves that will give you the opportunity to live the best life possible. I know that sounds like a lot of togetherness, but look at it this very simple way: You can't have too much togetherness if you're having fun.

You can't live the best life possible if you aren't your spouse's best friend, and you certainly won't live the best live available to you.

Premise # 19

You must pass this test with flying colors

Test Time

Okay, you've read the book and instead of tossing it, you're going to try to use some of the ideas which I've covered to improve your marriage and your life. If you've made that decision, I applaud you for the effort you're about to make, and I can tell you, if you stick with, it will be well worth your time.

However, before you start to work, I think it would be useful to find out where you stand. Maybe you know your marriage is on perilous ground, and you're not living the best life possible. On the other hand, maybe your marriage is just a little shaky, and you'd like to shore it up and enjoy a more fulfilling life. It could be that you have a vague idea of where some of your problems lie, but you're not sure. Either way, before you start to work on your marriage, you should evaluate where you are. That way you can concentrate on your weaknesses and see more improvement in a shorter period of time.

The test at the end of this chapter will help you pinpoint the weaknesses in your marriage. The next step is very important: You don't take the test; your spouse or significant other will take it for you and vice-versa. After you and your spouse take the test, you will have an honest appraisal of the marriage, and it will be obvious where the primary weaknesses are.

However, a word of caution: If you have seven or eight areas you need to work on, pick the most pressing one or two and focus on those. By doing so you'll be able to direct all your resources into one or two confined areas, and you'll have a much better chance of succeeding. If you try to address all seven or eight areas at the same time, you will very likely end up frustrated and accomplish very little.

After you have made a significant amount of progress on the first and second items, move to the next most pressing problem area. You'll find, after improving one part of your marriage, the second step will be much easier. Why? Because the quality of your life will show such an improvement that your desire to tackle the remainder of the items will increase.

However, as I mentioned earlier in this book, the quality life we are all seeking does not come easily. If you're drastically lacking in some of the categories I've listed, then prepare yourself for some real work, both physically and mentally. But believe me, it will be well worth the effort, if you can improve your marriage. After all, you spend more of your life with your marriage partner than with anyone else. Doesn't it make sense to do everything you can to improve the quality of life you live together?

More about the test: You'll notice the test applies directly to the key premises from each chapter, as they apply to your marriage and your life. After reading the book you and your spouse should have an idea of where you stand in relationship to the targeted emotional level sought in each chapter. Your spouse will fill in the blank at the end of each question, from 1 to 10, as to how they rate you, as to how you measure up when it comes to really surviving marriage. As you rate your spouse, consider the optimum level as outlined in the chapter that applies to the test. Consider that level, 10. Your score should reflect how close your marriage is to the optimum level.

For example: Is your marriage a true partnership? If you're a dominating general partner, and your spouse is a very limited partner, your spouse is going to give you a low score. Maybe 2 to 3 or even lower, depending on the situation. After you have given your spouse a score on every question—and don't leave out any—They will have an understanding of how you rate the marriage—from your point of view. The results are sometimes shocking, and if that's the case maybe your marriage needed that eye-opener. Of course, remember, your marriage partner has just done the same thing by taking this test and has rated you. Now, if both of you have been completely honest, the average of the two scores will tell you the approximately quality of your marriage.

The test is a vote by each marriage partner as to how they feel about the quality of every part of the marriage. They have evaluated their spouse by the ideal premise in this book. That's the current status of the marriage, as they see it. But more important, a closer look at the individual scores and the obvious points of weakness—low scores—will force the marriage partners to honestly evaluate the marriage. Sometimes a spouse will have rationalized for years that he or she was registering toward the top in many of these categories. To realize their spouse didn't feel that way at all is a blow to the ego—but it can be a positive one. The low scoring items are impossible to dismiss, and if used properly, can give impetus to a couple who wants to improve their marriage. This is a good time to remember the key premise of this book: Improving your marriage always leads to a better quality of life.

Now you have a work plan to improve your marriage. The whole point of this book is to provide a way to achieve the highest quality of life possible by improving your marriage. This test will show you where you are now and how to get to that higher plane. Look at the test questions where your spouse gave you a low score and remember, there's not a person in the world that understands you better than your spouse. If the person who knows you best, says you aren't measuring up in a category—you aren't. Don't try to second guess your spouse, but commit to take his or her assessment of the question. That's the only way you can move your marriage up to another level.

Remember, having a marriage that is in the top 5 percent of all marriages is a worthy goal. What could be better than living a joyous and pleasurable married life that 95 percent of the population never achieves?

One more suggestion before you rate your spouse. After you total your spouse's score, note it on the bottom of the page, and then bookmark this book where you can rate your spouse a year later. If, during the year, your spouse has worked on the items where they had the lowest score, you should see a marked improvement in their score, your marriage and quality of life.

THE MARRIAGE TEST

Rank your spouse from 1-10 where 10 is perfect for that attribute while a 1 means a good deal of work is required.

- Does your spouse treat you as an equal marriage partner?

- How do you rate your spouse sexually?

- Is your spouse fit?

- Is your spouse healthy?

- Does your spouse have a healthy lifestyle?

- Has your spouse kept up their appearance?

- How good is your spouse at giving gifts?

- Does your spouse value kids as a good part of your marriage?

- Does your spouse enjoy togetherness?

- Does your spouse have a good spiritual life?

- Is your spouse flexible and does he/she compromise?

- Does your spouse talk about everything?

- Does your spouse exhibit marriage honesty?

- Does your spouse accentuate the positive?

- Does your spouse touch, hug, kiss etc.?

- Is your spouse your best friend?

Your total score _____

Total your points and check the results below—**160 possible points**

Test analysis

160	The perfect marriage (you're dreaming!)
152	An exceptionally high quality marriage. You're in the top 5%. Pat yourself on the back.
128	A good strong marriage – but could stand some moderate improvement. You're in the top 20%.
112	Well above average – You're in the top 30%.
96	Above average but you have some critical marriage problems to solve. You're in the top 40% category
80	You need to make some drastic changes or the marriage won't last. You're in the 50% category.
64	Unless you make some changes, find a good lawyer. You're in the bottom 40% category.
16	This marriage is not working. You're in the bottom 10%.

A final word: By reading this book you've shown you care about your marriage and you want to improve it and live the best life possible. The premise of this book is very simple: A high quality marriage enables you to live the best life possible. If you believe this, then, by examining your marriage and applying the concepts listed in the various chapters, you can raise the quality of your marriage to a new level. It may be that your score is relatively good…maybe above 120. That's a good marriage, but even if you have a good quality marriage, there is always room for improvement.

Examine very closely how your spouse graded you in each individual chapter to determine where your weakness are and then tackle them. You'll find out that when you begin to shore up the weaknesses in your marriage, and every marriage has some, the result will be to move your the marriage relationship up in quality, to a more enjoyable level where you can enjoy the best life possible. The enjoyment and true pleasure you'll derive, if you move your marriage into the elite 95th percentile, will be worth a thousand times the effort.

You will live the best life possible.

Made in the USA
Monee, IL
04 November 2026

67382837R00138